DEEPENING YOUR
FAITH

Messages from the Gospel of John, Vol. II

DEEPENING YOUR
FAITH

Messages from the Gospel of John, Vol. II

GREG LAURIE

ALLEN
DAVID
BOOKS

KERYGMA™
PUBLISHING   Dana Point, California

Deepening Your Faith

ISBN 0-9762400-8-4

Printed in the United States of America.

Published by: Kerygma Publishing, Dana Point, California
Coordination: FM Management, Ltd.
Cover design: Christopher Laurie
Editing: Karla Pedrow
Interior Design: Highgate Cross+Cathey, Ltd.

Then they came to Philip,
who was from Bethsaida of
Galilee, and asked him, saying,
"Sir, we wish to see Jesus."

(John 12:21)

Contents

11

TIME FOR A
TEST

John 6: 1–14

I don't know about you, but I hated tests in school—especially those pop quizzes that I was not always prepared for. When it comes to tests, there is always that temptation to cheat. And plenty of students have given in to that temptation, like one little boy named Joshua, who was called to the front of the class by his history teacher.

His teacher said, "Joshua, I have reason to believe that you cheated on a test."

"Why would you think that?" Joshua asked.

"Well, you sat by Brittney during the test. And on question number one when it asked, 'Who was the first president of the United States?' Brittney wrote, 'George Washington.' You wrote, 'George Washington' also."

"But everyone knows that one!" Joshua said.

"Well, on question number two, it asks, 'Who wrote the Declaration of Independence?' Brittney wrote, 'Thomas Jefferson' as her answer," the teacher said, "and you did too, Josh."

"Everyone knows that one too," Joshua replied.

"It doesn't mean that I cheated."

His teacher continued, "The last question asked, 'Who was the seventeenth president of the United States?' and Brittney wrote, 'I don't know!' "

"So?"

"Joshua," his teacher said, "you wrote, 'Me either!' "

Tests. They are no fun, but they have their purpose, as James 1:2 reminds us:

> When all kind of trials and temptations crowd into your lives, my brothers, don't resent them as intruders, but welcome them as friends! Realise [sic] that they come to test your faith and to produce in you the quality of endurance. But let the process go on until that endurance is fully developed, and you will find you have become men of mature character, men of integrity with no weak spots. (PHILLIPS)

In John 6, we find a series of tests, or pop quizzes, if you will, that Jesus sprung on His disciples to see if they were listening, learning, and paying attention. He was preparing them for the future, because He wanted them to become what the above passage in James describes:

> "men of mature character, men of integrity with no weak spots."

We see the first of such tests in the feeding of the five thousand, the one and only miracle that is mentioned in all four Gospels. Clearly, God wants us to learn from this, because He gave it to us in quadraphonic.

—————⋙◆◈◆⋘—————

God doesn't want to be thought of as a celestial "Big Buddy."

—————⋙◆◈◆⋘—————

At this point in His ministry, Jesus was on a roll. His fame was growing by the minute. The crowds swelled wherever He went. Multitudes of people anxiously followed Him. Judging by the criteria of many churches today, these factors alone would demonstrate that His ministry was an unqualified success. It doesn't matter why or for what people come, just as long as they come. It is all in the numbers. At least, that's how some see things.

But for Jesus, motive and purpose were everything. We see this earlier in John 2:

> Now when He was in Jerusalem at the Passover, during the feast, many believed in His name when they saw the signs which He did. But Jesus did not commit Himself to them, because He knew all men, and had no need that anyone should testify of man, for He knew what was in man. (vv. 23–25)

Though they believed in Him, Jesus didn't believe in them. And though many trusted Him, He didn't trust in them. Why? Because He knew what was in them. Jesus sees us for what we are, not for what we think we are. There are no secrets with Him. He is "the searcher of hearts" (see Rom. 8:27) and the One who knows hearts. And according to Jeremiah 17:9, "The human heart is most deceitful and desperately wicked. Who really knows how bad it is?" (NLT).

God wants us to realize that all we have comes from Him.

In time, Jesus would directly challenge these people and intentionally say things with the purpose of thinning out the ranks. God doesn't want to be thought of as a celestial "Big Buddy," someone we claim to follow because it helps us feel better about ourselves or because we think we need a little religion in our lives. He wants us to follow Him because we love Him and want to know Him.

The reason these people followed Jesus was clear. It was not necessarily because they knew He was their long-awaited Messiah. Many of these people were nothing more than thrill seekers. John tells us that "a huge crowd kept following him wherever he went, because they saw his miracles as he healed the sick" (6:2 NLT). And according to Matthew's Gospel, as Jesus surveyed the massive crowd, which numbered as high as ten thousand people (including women and children), He knew their motive—but He had compassion on them in spite of it (see Matt. 9:36). Even though He knew these were shallow, thrill-seeking people, Jesus was deeply moved as He looked at them. Jesus, better than anyone, knew their fickleness, and He knew they would soon reject Him. Yet His heart burned for them.

Now, if I had been there with these multitudes and had known what Jesus knew, I would have been very tempted to let them starve. After all, if I knew at that moment that some of the very people I was feeding would, in a short time, join the jeers of the crowds who were crying, "Crucify Him!" I wouldn't have given these people the time of day, much less a free lunch. (I'm glad that I am not omniscient like Jesus is.)

In addition to Jesus, there are three people specifically mentioned in this text: Philip, Andrew, and a little boy.

THE FIRST TEST

First, there is Philip. It appears that among the twelve disciples, Philip was the apostolic administrator—the road manager, so to speak. It looked as though Philip was in charge of arranging meals and logistics. He seemed to possess the classic traits and personality of an administrator. So, surrounded by these massive crowds and seeing they were hungry, Jesus turned to His disciple Philip and gave the first test. Jesus wanted to see if Philip's faith had been stretched, so He asked Him a question. Which, by the way, is the only record of Jesus ever asking a person for advice: "Where shall we buy bread, that these may eat?" (John 6:5).

Philip did not really answer the Lord's question, but responded with some statistics: "Two hundred denarii worth of bread is not sufficient for them, that every one of them may have a little" (v. 7). In other words, "It would take a small fortune to feed them, Lord!"

Philip seemed to fail the Lord's test because he was too reliant on his own understanding and abilities. Philip saw the situation only through the eyes of logic. Now, that is not to say that logic and faith are incompatible. In fact, I think some people could use a lot more of each. But Philip simply did not see the possibilities. He was responsible, honest, and at times, lacking in faith. He needed to set aside his materialistic, pragmatic, common-sense concerns and learn to lay hold of the supernatural potential of faith. So it would appear that Philip sadly failed this test.

THE SECOND TEST

Next we come to Andrew. Originally introduced to Jesus by John the Baptist, Andrew was a devoted disciple of John's—that is, until one day John saw Jesus walk by and said, "Behold! The Lamb of God who takes away the sin of the world!" (John 1:29). Right away, Andrew found his brother Simon Peter and told him, "We have found the Messiah" (v. 41).

Andrew was very spiritually perceptive. He was always bringing others to Jesus. We celebrate the Simon Peters of the world and often forget the Andrews. But remember, there would be no Simon Peters if there were no Andrews.

So Andrew, true to form, turned to Jesus and said, "There is a lad here who has five barley loaves and two small fish, but what are they among so many?" (John 6:9). Andrew had the right idea in mentioning this little boy and his lunch. But doubt caught up with him: *But what are they among so many?* Though faring better than the doubtful Philip, Andrew missed the point and at best got a passing grade on the test Jesus gave.

THE THIRD TEST

Then there was the little boy. What do we know about this little guy? First of all, we know that he was poor. His lunch was largely composed of barley bread. This is significant, because it was the least expensive of all bread and generally was looked upon with contempt, because it was thought of as food for animals, not people. In addition to the loaves of barley bread, the boy had two small fish. The modern equivalent would be something along the lines of sardines and crackers (and stale crackers at that).

Yet this boy did something that set him apart from all other boys who may have been in the crowd that day. This boy gave his lunch, as meager as it was, to Jesus. The boy was as insignificant as he could be. His lunch was as insignificant as it could be. But that which was *insufficient* in the hands of the *insignificant* became *sufficient* and *significant* when placed in the hands of Jesus.

We see this throughout the pages of Scripture. God takes the insignificant and makes it significant.

What is as insignificant as dust? You can't even plant crops in dust. Yet dust became a man when molded by the hands of the Creator.

The jawbone of a donkey is pretty insignificant. But God used it in the hands of Samson to defeat one thousand enemies of Israel.

A shepherd's rod is insignificant, yet when God placed it in the hands of Moses, it became a powerful instrument used to deliver the Israelites from centuries of bondage in Egypt.

A sling is unimportant, but God used it in the hands of David to kill the mighty Goliath.

And what is as insignificant as a poor virgin in a distant town of the Roman Empire? Yet God took that young girl named Mary and used her to bring into the world the Savior of all.

So do not make the mistake of believing that what you have is insignificant and therefore useless. You may compare your gifts and abilities with all the great talents of this world (at least those whom you think are great) and think that your gift is worthless. But if you see it that way, you are missing something.

What is it that makes a gift great in God's service? It is not the magnitude of the gift, but it is into whose hands the gift is given. I could pick up a guitar and play it, and you would think it is almost worthless. You might think, "That guitar is a piece of junk!" The fact is that the one who is playing the guitar is lacking in skill. But if an experienced musician picked up the same guitar, you would think it was a choice instrument.

Which seems larger in your eyes: God or your problems?

It is like the auctioneer who was selling an old violin, and couldn't even get someone to bid five dollars for it. Then an elderly man made his way to the front. He took the old, weathered violin and blew the dust off. After carefully tuning it, he took the bow in his hand and began to play a complex, classical piece. The beautiful music filled the room. When he was finished, the man laid down the violin and returned to his seat. The auctioneer picked up the violin once again and said, "Do I hear one thousand dollars?"

Afterward, a woman approached the auctioneer and asked, "Why is it that this violin, which fifteen minutes earlier could not be sold for five dollars, has sold for more than two thousand?"

"That's easy," the auctioneer told her. "It was the touch of the master's hand."

So bring your fish and loves (or your stale crackers and sardines) and present them to Jesus. Bring your life, your strengths, and yes, your weaknesses, and see what the touch of the Master's hand can bring about.

So Philip failed the Lord's test, and Andrew perhaps got a passing grade. But the little boy? He got an "A." Let me say one more thing about Andrew, however. While he did not pass Jesus' test with flying colors, he did bring the little boy to Jesus. He basically said, "I don't have anything to offer, but I know someone who does!" You might be an Andrew for someone else whom you can encourage to use his or her gift to serve the Lord.

BELIEVING GOD FOR THE IMPOSSIBLE

The test Jesus gave His disciples was to see whether they believed He could meet their needs, even when it seemed impossible. When Jesus taught the disciples to pray, He told them, "In this manner, therefore, pray: 'Our Father in heaven, hallowed

be Your name. … Give us this day our daily bread' "
(Matt. 6:9, 11). God wants us to realize that all we
have comes from Him, and we are to look to Him
for our provision. But there will be times when that
provision will not come as quickly as we would like.
Have you ever been in a situation where you had no
food to eat or any money to pay your bills? I have.

> *God will allow us to
> enter into situations in which
> the only way out is Him.*

Are you in such a situation right now? Do you
feel there is no other place to look but up? I can
say that, after walking with the Lord for more than
thirty years, He has always provided for my needs,
as Philippians 4:19 promises: "And my God shall
supply all your need according to His riches in
glory by Christ Jesus." Notice this doesn't say that
God will supply all our *greeds*. But it does say that
He will provide for all our *needs*. God is still in the
miracle business.

Maybe this is why it doesn't seem to have
occurred to the disciples that Jesus could
miraculously feed them. After all, they had seen
a number of dramatic miracles at this point, from

water being turned into wine to a lame man being healed. Was it because they thought that feeding these people was too trivial—or somehow too much of a challenge? Nothing is too hard for the Lord (see Gen. 18:14), yet at the same time, He is interested in the smallest of matters, as the psalmist reminds us: "You keep track of all my sorrows. You have collected all my tears in your bottle. You have recorded each one in your book. On the very day I call to you for help, my enemies will retreat. This I know: God is on my side" (Psalm 56:8–9 NLT).

The disciples had a defective view of Jesus. That was their problem, and it is very often our problem too. And in the Old Testament, we see a similar problem with the nation of Israel. Years before David became king, Israel departed from God's plan for them (a theocracy under judges) and decided they wanted to be like other nations that were ruled by kings. So they chose Saul, the tallest man in the nation. Had there been such a thing back then, Saul would have won the People's Choice Award. He just looked like a king, the Israelites thought. So they chose the giant in their nation to be their ruler, only to find themselves cowering awhile later before another giant, Goliath, from the enemy army of the Philistines.

Then along came David. In contrast to the majority of his countrymen, David did not have a defective concept of God. According to 1 Samuel 17, when David saw Israel's armies retreating before Goliath, he asked, "Who is this pagan Philistine anyway, that he is allowed to defy the armies of the living God?" (v. 26 NLT). He did not see God in the light of Goliath; instead, he saw Goliath in the light of God. David, the shepherd boy, told Saul, the giant of Israel,

> "When a lion or a bear comes to steal a lamb from the flock, I go after it with a club and take the lamb from its mouth. If the animal turns on me, I catch it by the jaw and club it to death. I have done this to both lions and bears, and I'll do it to this pagan Philistine, too, for he has defied the armies of the living God! The Lord who saved me from the claws of the lion and the bear will save me from this Philistine!" (vv. 35–36 NLT)

David had the right concept of God, demonstrated by the fact that he ran *toward* Goliath as he called upon the Lord.

Who or what seems too much for you to handle today? Which seems larger in your eyes: God or your problems? Like David, we should not see God in the light of our problems, but our problems in the light of God.

God takes the insignificant and makes it significant.

Jesus now proves there is nothing too big or too small for Him to do. Mark 6 provides us with some detail regarding what Jesus did first:

> Then He commanded them to make them all sit down in groups on the green grass. So they sat down in ranks, in hundreds and in fifties. And when He had taken the five loaves and the two fish, He looked up to heaven, blessed and broke the loaves, and gave them to His disciples to set before them; and the two fish He divided among them all. So they all ate and were filled. And they took up twelve baskets full of fragments and of the fish. Now those who had eaten the loaves were about five thousand men. (vv. 39–44)

Jesus blessed what He had, and as they distributed it, it just kept multiplying. In other words, the loaves and the fish did not explode into a mountain of food. It probably appeared to be the same amount. They simply could not exhaust it.

The same is true for us. God gives us what we need when we need it—not necessarily before, and never after, but when it is needed. So, take what you have and start working with it, because gifts from God seldom come fully developed. Sometimes we are waiting for a fully mature and developed gift to drop into our lives. But that takes time.

When I was boy, we once had a guest in our home who was an artist for Disney. I watched in amazement and admiration as he seemed to effortlessly sketch out Disney characters one after the other, right before my eyes. Our guest told me that he could draw this way because of his magic pencil. And much to my delight, he gave his magic pencil to me before he left.

God is still in the miracle business.

It didn't take long for me to discover there was nothing magical about that pencil, however. The so-called magic amounted to many hours of practice the artist had put in to develop his talent.

The apostle Paul urged the young pastor, Timothy, to "fan into flames the spiritual gift God gave you when I laid my hands on you" (2 Tim. 1:6 NLT). Also speaking of spiritual gifts, Paul wrote,

God has given each of us the ability to do certain things well. So if God has given you the ability to prophesy, speak out when you have faith that God is speaking through you. If your gift is that of serving others, serve them well. If you are a teacher, do a good job of teaching. If your gift is to encourage others, do it! If you have money, share it generously. If God has given you leadership ability, take the responsibility seriously. And if you have a gift for showing kindness to others, do it gladly. (Rom. 12:6–8 NLT)

As we use the gifts God has given us, no matter how feeble or small in our sight they may be, God will develop and even multiply them.

A TALE OF TWO AGENDAS

I want to point out one final thing about this miracle Jesus performed. There was no swelling music in the background or Hollywood special effects that accompanied what Jesus did. Instead, there was a calm set of directions:

Then Jesus said, 'Make the people sit down.' Now there was much grass in the place. So the men sat down, in number about five thousand. And Jesus took the loaves, and when He had given thanks He distributed them to the disciples, and the disciples to those sitting down; and likewise of the fish, as much as they wanted. (John 6:10–11)

God often does His greatest work in quiet ways. We saw this when Jesus turned water into wine at the wedding in Cana. We see it in the Old Testament account of Elijah, after his dramatic showdown with the prophets of Baal on Mount Carmel:

> Then He said, "Go out, and stand on the mountain before the Lord." And behold, the Lord passed by, and a great and strong wind tore into the mountains and broke the rocks in pieces before the Lord, but the Lord was not in the wind; and after the wind an earthquake, but the Lord was not in the earthquake; and after the earthquake a fire, but the Lord was not in the fire; and after the fire a still small voice. So it was, when Elijah heard it, that he wrapped his face in his mantle and went out and stood in the entrance of the cave. (1 Kings 19:11–13)

We find a lot of drama in the above passage: strong winds, an earthquake, and a fire, yet God was not in any of these things. The Lord came with a still, small voice. And that is how God will usually come to us.

Without question, the feeding of the five thousand became the most popular miracle that Jesus had performed. Even so, the people had another agenda altogether. John tells us:

> Then those men, when they had seen the sign that Jesus did, said, "This is truly the Prophet who is to come into the world." Therefore when Jesus perceived that they were about to come and take Him by force to make Him king, He departed again to a mountain by Himself alone. (6:14–15)

The whole idea of taking Jesus by force is laughable. It was not any different than putting Jesus in chains at His arrest. No one could take His life; He laid it down of His own accord. These people wanted to *use* God instead of be *used by* Him. At that time, they lived under Roman occupation. They wanted their freedom again. They thought, "If we could get Jesus on our side, we could drive out the Romans."

Sometimes, we Christians do the same thing. We want God to do what *we* want Him to do. Politicians will invoke His name in the hopes of being elected to office. (I would recommend checking their record instead to see if they have voted for the values you believe in rather than just accepting their rhetoric.) Salespeople will speak of God if they think it will help them get a sale: "Oh, are *you* a Christian? I am too! Say, bro, help me out here!" Others will use Jesus in hopes of starting a relationship with an attractive guy or girl: "Oh, yes, I'm a Christian too. So how about one of those holy kisses?"

> *God often does His greatest work in quiet ways.*

But Jesus will not be used by people. He will walk away, just as He did from the multitudes He had just fed. Even so, He can *use* people for His glory if they are willing for Him to do so.

So what can we learn from this story?

First, we can realize there will come situations in life in which we have neither the resources nor the ability to respond. There will be things that are beyond our control. These are the tests I was referring to at the beginning of this chapter, and God gives us these tests to determine whether we are learning anything as Christians.

The way to pass this test is to see our utter inability to do anything about these situations on

our own. Instead, we are to come to God and cast
ourselves on Him and Him alone for the answer.
There is no back-up plan—just plain trust in God.
When that unexpected bill comes in the mail and
you wonder, "How will we ever pay this?"; when
there is a crisis with your spouse and you think,
"How will we ever get through this?"; when your
"perfect" child gets himself into trouble and you
ask, "How will we survive this?"; when there is that
problem at work and you say to yourself, "I don't
think I can make it another day," can you trust
God? You must. God will allow us to enter into
situations in which the only way out is Him. Then
He will get the glory.

We find such a situation in the Old Testament
story of King Jehoshaphat. His enemies, who
greatly outnumbered him, had joined forces and
were coming to destroy him and his people. When
he heard the news, his heart sank, and he was
filled with fear. Have you ever had that happen?
Have you ever been in a situation that looks utterly
hopeless?

Jehoshaphat could have panicked or thrown
a temper tantrum. But the Bible tells us that
Jehoshaphat "set himself to seek the Lord, and

proclaimed a fast throughout all Judah" (2 Chron. 20:3). Then he prayed before all the people, " 'O our God, will You not judge them? For we have no power against this great multitude that is coming against us; nor do we know what to do, but our eyes are upon You' " (v. 12). And guess what happened? God delivered them.

God gives us what we need when we need it.

Second, we need to remember that nothing is too big or even too small for God to respond to. The psalmist penned this prayer: "Hear my cry, O God; attend to my prayer. From the end of the earth I will cry to You, when my heart is overwhelmed; lead me to the rock that is higher than I" (Ps. 61:1–2). And 1 Peter 5:7 says to "give all your worries and cares to God, for he cares about what happens to you" (NLT). When we are overwhelmed, when we are worried and discouraged, we need to look at God's greatness— not the size of our problems.

Third, we are to bring our talents, abilities, gifts, and resources to Jesus. No matter how insignificant they may seem to you, God can use whatever you bring to Him. Think of the supposedly insignificant people God has used throughout history. Joseph was only a slave, but God used him to save both Egypt and Israel (see Gen. 45:3–7). He used a young slave girl to bring the powerful Syrian General, Naaman, to the prophet Elisha for healing (see 2 Kings 5). And He used a formally ostracized, immoral woman to bring a town to faith (see John 4:1–42).

It has been said that big doors swing on small hinges. So if you're tempted to believe that you are too insignificant to be used of God, remember that you can never be too small for God to use—only too big.

HURRICANE
GRACE

John 6: 15–21

I n our fifteen-year history of Harvest Crusades, which are large-evangelistic events that we hold around the world, we have, for the most part, been blessed with good weather. But on three occasions, we have had our crusades interrupted by storms in Colorado, Florida, and Hawaii. During our 1992 crusade in Honolulu, the arrival of Hurricane Iniki forced us to cancel one night of the crusade. Three years later, we were holding a crusade in Colorado Springs when a September blizzard swept across Colorado's Front Range, dropping the temperature from 70 degrees to 20 degrees in the outdoor stadium. Needless to say, attendance was significantly down that night. The following month in Ft. Lauderdale, we were drenched by a tropical storm from Hurricane Roxanne.

You never know when a storm will come, and the same can be true for the storms of life.

Sometimes out of nowhere, we find ourselves facing a difficult or broken relationship, a financial crisis, legal problems, or painful health issues. Maybe it is the death of someone we love. Maybe it is a rebellious child. Maybe it is the loss of a job. Maybe it is a conflict at work or at church. At some time in our lives, we will all face these kinds of storms. In fact, there are only two kinds of people in the world: those who are *going* through a crisis, and those who are *going to go* through a crisis.

If we want to go sailing on the open seas of God's leading, then we will face storms.

You may remember the film, *The Perfect Storm*, about the storm that hit off the coast of Gloucester, Massachusetts in October 1991. Stronger than any other storm in recorded history, it was called "the perfect storm," because it was three storms combined into one, creating an almost apocalyptic situation in the Atlantic. Two existing storms converged with a hurricane, ironically labeled Hurricane Grace, to form a monstrous, two-thousand-mile-wide hurricane, in which boats encountered waves one hundred feet high—the equivalent of a ten-story building.

Here before us is a story of the disciples being hit by a Hurricane Grace, so to speak. While very difficult to endure, this storm would yield some important lessons for them. In effect, it was "the perfect storm."

Let's read about it:

> Therefore when Jesus perceived that they were about to come and take Him by force to make Him king, He departed again to the mountain by Himself alone. Now when evening came, His disciples went down to the sea, got into the boat, and went over the sea toward Capernaum. And it was already dark, and Jesus had not come to them. Then the sea arose because a great wind was blowing. So when they had rowed about three or four miles, they saw Jesus walking on the sea and drawing near the boat; and they were afraid. But He said to them, "It is I; do not be afraid." (John 6:15–20)

Matthew's Gospel tells us that Jesus made the disciples get into this boat and go to the other side of the Sea of Galilee (see Matt. 14:22). Why? He did it for their own good. Jesus had just performed His most popular miracle to date, the Feeding of the Five Thousand. As we learned from the previous chapter, this miracle prompted the people to attempt to "take Him by force to make Him king" (v. 15).

I personally think the disciples were pretty excited about this entire prospect. After all, if Jesus were king, then they, as His adopted family, would be royalty as well. The situation was much like children having a good time and then being told by their parents to get in the car. The disciples probably did not want to leave.

But Jesus wanted to diffuse this movement to make Him king. At this point, it was a worst-case scenario for the disciples. They had the potential of going from suffering indifference and indignity to ruling over the people. They would become powerful and respected. It was a rags-to-riches story in the making. And that's exactly why Jesus had to get them out of town—as soon as possible. He knew this would have destroyed these disciples, who were known for their jockeying for position and arguing over who would get the best seat at the table.

Besides, this was not how Jesus was to be crowned as king. He was not here on Earth to set up a kingdom ruled by human power. He was here to establish the kingdom of God that would rule in the hearts of men and women.

———⊙⊙⊙———

God's delays are not necessarily God's denials.

———⊙⊙⊙———

So off these disciples had to go. In Matthew's version of this event, we read that *"Immediately* Jesus made His disciples get into the boat" (14:22, emphasis mine), which strongly suggests they did not want to leave.

Did Jesus know a storm was waiting for them? Yes. But He would use it for their benefit. In the same way, sometimes the things we dread the most can actually be the best for us.

The disciples also may have noticed that a storm was brewing on the lake. But in obedience to Jesus' command, they began rowing. However, they hit a very strong wind. If only they had turned in the direction of the wind. Then they would reach the shore. But Jesus had told them to "go before Him to the other side" (Matt. 14:22), and that is exactly what they were going to do. This reminds us that the place of security is not always the place of easy circumstances, but the place of obedience to the will of God.

LESSON ONE: GOD WILL SEND STORMS INTO OUR LIVES

There are several things we can learn from the disciples' encounter with "the perfect storm," the first of them being the fact that God will send storms into our lives.

Of course, there are storms that come our way as a result of our own disobedience, like the type Jonah faced when he disobeyed God and tried to run. A great storm came, and the Lord took hold of this reluctant prophet and got him back on course. This storm was entirely the result of Jonah's own disobedience to God and His call on his life.

But there are also storms that can come from our own obedience. Moses, for example, never would have needed to put up with a large contingent of complaining people had he not obeyed God at the burning bush. He could have simply stayed with his little flock of sheep in the desert, and we never would have known his name or been inspired by his story.

Daniel never would have faced a lion's den had he not been faithful to God.

Shadrach, Meshach, and Abed-Nego never would have had to face a fiery furnace if they simply had bowed to the gold image that King Nebuchadnezzar set up. Then again, if they had bowed, they would have missed the privilege of experiencing Jesus' presence in the fire with them.

Are we eagerly waiting for Him?

These people all got through their storms, and now we see the victories they won for the Kingdom. Sure, we can play it safe and stay tucked in our own little harbor. But if we want to go sailing on the open seas of God's leading, then we will face storms.

The bad news is that storms are inevitable. But the good new is that, as a Christian, you will learn through them and experience great victories. And there's more good news: storms don't last forever.

One person who weathered the storms in his life beautifully was Joseph. Years had passed since his brothers had betrayed him and literally sold him out by selling him to Egyptian slave traders. They probably thought he was dead. But Joseph was very much alive. Not only that, there was a famine going on, and he was in charge of the food supply for the civilized world. When Joseph's brothers were called into his court, they didn't even recognize him. But Joseph knew them. And he called them close and dropped a bombshell: "I am Joseph, your brother whom you sold into Egypt. But don't be angry with yourselves that you did this to me, for God did it. He sent me here ahead of you to preserve your lives" (Gen. 45:4–5 NLT). "God did it"—that is in amazing statement. Joseph didn't say, "God allowed it." He simply said, "God did it." His brothers couldn't believe their ears. But Joseph knew that God was in control of everything that had happened to him.

This gives us the big picture when it comes to life's storms. As believers, whatever happens in our lives is either something that God has allowed or is doing. We are familiar with the words of Romans 8:28: "And we know that all things work together for good to those who love God, to those who are the called according to His purpose." But we also need to remember the verse that follows it: "For whom He foreknew, He also predestined to be conformed to the image of His Son, that He might be the firstborn among many brethren" (v. 29). What this is saying is that what happens in our lives will always ultimately work for our good in that it will make us more like Jesus. In other words, although we are interested in what is *temporarily* good, God is interested in what is *eternally* good. He is looking at the long-term to make us more like the Lord Jesus himself.

When we focus on Christ, we begin to find and receive His help.

It reminds me of when I was a young boy and lived with my grandparents, Mama Stella and Daddy Charles. They were from Arkansas, so I ate good Southern cooking like fried chicken, black-eyed peas, collard greens, and mashed potatoes for dinner almost every night. Mama Stella believed in making every meal from scratch, and we never had leftovers. Her biscuits, however, were her crowning culinary achievement. I have never had a better biscuit made by anyone, anywhere. I used to watch her make them. She used vegetable oil, self-rising flour, and buttermilk. Of course, no ingredient she used for her mouthwatering biscuits was appealing to me on its own. But when she mixed all the ingredients together with expert hands and put them into a hot oven, the result was one good biscuit.

In the same way, when God takes the events of our lives—the good things and the so-called bad things—and puts them into the oven of adversity, when it is all done, we say, "That is good." It may take time. And it may even take a lifetime.

A lifetime is what it must have felt like to the disciples as they battled the storm there on the Sea of Galilee. They might have felt that Jesus had somehow forgotten them.

LESSON TWO: NOTHING ESCAPES GOD'S ATTENTION

But Jesus was watching. And this leads us to the second thing we can learn from the disciples' encounter with this storm: nothing escapes God's attention. We may lose sight of Him, but He never loses sight of us.

"Where is He?" the disciples may have wondered. But He was watching their every move (and I'm sure He was also praying). Mark 6:48 tells us, "Then He saw them straining at rowing, for the wind was against them. ... " Jesus never lost sight of the disciples, even though He was on the mountain and they were on the sea. Has it ever seemed to you as though you were all alone in your storm and that no one sees you? God sees you. As Proverbs 15:3 tells us, "The eyes of the Lord are in every place, keeping watch on the evil and the good." Just as surely as Jesus was praying for the disciples, He is praying and interceding for us too. According to Romans 8:34, "It is Christ who died, and furthermore is also risen, who is even at the right hand of God, who also makes intercession for us." And we find this promise in Hebrews 7:25: "Therefore He is also able to save to the uttermost those who come to God through Him, since He always lives to make intercession for them." So it wasn't that Jesus had forgotten about them, nor was He late. Because as surely as God has His will, He also has His timing.

Consider the case of Lazarus. Upon hearing that His friend was sick, Jesus delayed His arrival until Lazarus was dead. When Jesus finally arrived in Bethany, both Martha and Mary accused Him of failure (see John 11:21, 32). But Jesus had not failed. And He wasn't late. While they wanted a healing, Jesus wanted a resurrection.

In the same way, we sometimes wonder,

"Where is Jesus?" We look at the state of our wicked world today and perhaps wonder, "When is He coming to execute judgment?" But as 2 Peter 3:9 reminds us, "The Lord is not slow in keeping his promise, as some understand slowness. He is patient with you, not wanting anyone to perish, but everyone to come to repentance" (NIV). So let's not mistake God's timing for God's indifference. God sees us in the storm. And He will intervene in His own time and according to His own plan.

LESSON THREE: JESUS HELPS US IN OUR STORMS

The third thing we can learn from this "perfect storm" in which the disciples found themselves is that Jesus helps us in our storms. Matthew tells us that it was in the fourth watch of the night that Jesus came to them (see Matt. 14:25). The fourth watch was the time just before dawn, meaning that the disciples had been at sea for at least nine hours, most of that time in this fierce storm.

This just goes to show that God's delays are not necessarily God's denials. Jesus knew what He was doing all along. But why did He wait so long before He intervened? I think it was probably because He knew how long it would take for the disciples to exhaust their resources so they would completely trust in Him.

As a longtime resident of Southern California, I enjoy spending time at the beach. As a result, I have had the opportunity to see lifeguards at work. Any lifeguard knows there is a certain timing associated with saving the life of someone who is drowning. If a lifeguard approaches too soon, he or she can be pulled under by a panicked swimmer. A wise lifeguard will wait until someone is nearly exhausted before coming to his or her aid. In the same way, God will sometimes allow us to come to the end of ourselves and our resources so that we will learn to trust in Him, because when we get to the end of ourselves, we get to the beginning of God.

Not only was Jesus' timing important as He came to the disciples in the midst of the storm, but His method was important as well. Verse 19 tells us, "So when they had rowed about three or four miles, they saw Jesus walking on the sea and drawing near the boat; and they were afraid." Now why would Jesus come walking on the water? Why not just fly in, or suddenly appear in the boat? I think He wanted to show His disciples that the very things they feared, the wind and the sea, were only a staircase for Him to use to come to them. But this scared them even more. Matthew tells us they thought Jesus was a ghost (see Matt. 14:26).

I would much rather try and fail than to never do anything at all.

Why didn't the disciples recognize this was Jesus? It was because they weren't looking for Him. Had they been waiting in faith, they would have recognized Jesus immediately. Instead, they jumped to the false conclusion that this was a ghost. But there Jesus was, in the place they had least expected Him.

How often does the Lord speak to us, wanting to lead us, yet we don't see Him, because we aren't looking for Him? So much is happening in our world today, from terrorism to war to political instability and the threat of nuclear conflict. Yet Jesus said, "When these things begin to happen, look up and lift up your heads, because your redemption draws near" (Luke 21:28). We are to be looking for Jesus, as Hebrews 9:28 reminds us: "To those who eagerly wait for Him He will appear a second time, apart from sin, for salvation." As believers, we know that Jesus is coming again. But are we looking for Him? Are we eagerly waiting for Him?

We have a German shepherd who likes to sleep just outside our bedroom door at night. Or perhaps it would be more accurate to say that he leans against our door. When I open the door in the morning, he comes rolling in. Then he jumps up, tail wagging, ready for me to take him for a walk. He has been eagerly waiting for me to appear. All night long, he knew that his master would arrive at that door in the morning.

Where faith reigns,
fear has no place.

That is how our attitude should be toward the return of Jesus Christ. Are you looking for Him right now? Are you eagerly awaiting His arrival? You may know Jesus, but you never will know Him deeply until He comes to you in the midst of the storms of life. That was Job's conclusion after all the calamity that befell him: "My ears had heard of you but now my eyes have seen you" (Job 42:5 NIV). In other words, "I have heard how you deliver people and answer prayer. *Now* I know."

The disciples were about to know Jesus more deeply as He came to them in the midst of this perfect storm. As they froze in fear at the sight of Him, His reassuring voice pierced the darkness: "It is I; do not be afraid" (v. 20). Note the order of the words. He didn't say, "Do not be afraid" before He said, "It is I." It reminds us that when we focus on Christ, we begin to find and receive His help. The disciples' fear had given way to faith. They knew it was Jesus, and they knew they would be all right.

As Jesus reassured them, Peter suddenly experienced a great burst of faith in his heart. He was filled with love and devotion for the Lord, and he just wanted to be near Him. Peter had gone from terror to boldness. Jesus had said, "Do not be afraid," and now Peter was ready to prove his courage. He was ready to do the impossible. Matthew's account fills us in:

> And Peter answered Him and said, "Lord,
> if it is You, command me to come to You on
> the water." So He said, "Come." And when
> Peter had come down out of the boat, he
> walked on the water to go to Jesus. But when
> he saw that the wind was boisterous, he was
> afraid; and beginning to sink he cried out,

saying, "Lord, save me!" And immediately Jesus stretched out His hand and caught him, and said to him, "O you of little faith, why did you doubt?" (Matt. 14:28–31)

So there was Peter, walking on the water. He could do this because he was looking at Jesus.

I remember when I took my son scuba diving in Hawaii for the first time. After we had gone through the training with the instructor, it was time for a real dive. But on that particular day, the waters were very rough. Jonathan looked at me, panicked. The instructor, sensing Jonathan's fear, turned to him and very calmly but firmly said, "Look at me, and remember what I told you!" Jonathan relaxed, and as soon as we went below the surface, we discovered that all was calm.

Do you think Peter's failure came as a surprise to Jesus?

That is how it was with Peter too. When Peter took his eyes off Jesus, things fell apart: "But when he saw that the wind was boisterous, he was afraid; and beginning to sink he cried out, saying, 'Lord, save me!' " (v. 30).

So after Peter's great success came failure. But it was a spectacular failure. After all, if you are going to fail, then this is the way to do it. Have you ever tried to do something for God that turned out to be a complete failure? Maybe it was an attempt to share the gospel with someone. Perhaps it was a prayer for someone to get better, and the person actually got worse. (This has happened to me!) Or maybe you started a home Bible study and no one showed up. If so, then let me say this: thank you for failures.

I would much rather try and fail than to never do anything at all. Besides, failure is not always such a bad thing, because it is often failure that precedes success. We learn from our mistakes. And failure can indeed teach success. Often the doorway to success has been entered through the hallway of failure. It has been said that if at first you don't succeed, relax. You're just like the rest of us.

There are many who failed initially, only to succeed later. Albert Einstein failed at math before he realized e = mc². An apple had to fall on Isaac Newton's head before he discovered the theory of gravity. And Michael Jordan failed to make his high school basketball team, only to later make the NBA and become a sports legend.

So Peter's great fear turned to faith and then back to fear again. Where faith reigns, fear has no place. Where fear reigns, faith is driven away. Fear is a powerful and very real emotion that can suddenly overtake us. Verse 30 tells us, "And beginning to sink he [Peter] cried out. ... " Now up to this point, Peter was doing well. *Really* well. What he was doing was nothing short of amazing! But then He took His eyes off Jesus and put them elsewhere. In his case, it was the wind. In our case, it can be something else.

When we take our eyes off God, we forget His promises to us. We forget that He is in control of our lives. We forget Him altogether. And then we start to sink. Maybe you are sinking right now. Maybe you feel like a complete failure, because there was a time when you were so strong spiritually. God was using you. You were praying and seeing answers to your prayers. But then you took your eyes off Jesus and started longing toward the passing things of this world again. Or maybe it was not anything outwardly sinful that drew your eyes away from the Lord. Perhaps it was your career or a relationship or some pursuit that became more important to you than your faith. And now you are sinking. So is this the end? Absolutely not. You should do exactly what Peter did. He cried out to Jesus: "And beginning to sink, he cried out, saying, 'Lord, save me!' " (Matt. 14:30).

Notice that Peter prayed as he was *beginning* to sink. Better that than to wait until he had already sunk. There is no shame in that. In fact, it was good thinking. Crying out to God when you're in trouble does not mean that you are a big disappointment to God somehow. God is not disillusioned with you. He never had any illusions about you. Nor does it mean that you are worthless. It simply means that you have learned a thing or two in life. And one of those things is that when you start sinking, you need to pray.

In reality, do you think Peter's failure came as a surprise to Jesus? Do you think Jesus was shocked when Peter sank—or when he later denied Him? Of course He wasn't.

LESSON FOUR: JESUS WON'T LET US SINK

So the fourth thing we can learn from the disciples and the perfect storm is that Jesus won't let us sink. He will always rescue us—that is, if we call out to Him.

"And immediately Jesus stretched out His hand

and caught him, and said to him, 'O you of little
faith, why did you doubt?' " (Matt. 14:31). The
phrase, "little faith" is actually translated from
one word in the original Greek, a word that has
a quality of tenderness about it. It was as though
Jesus were saying to Peter, "Oh, *Littlefaith*, you
were doing so well! What happened?" And guess
what? With his eyes back on Jesus, "Littlefaith"
walked back to the boat. In other words, Peter
walked on the water again. We don't read that the
storm stopped until they reached the boat: "And
when they got into the boat, the wind ceased"
(v. 32). The storm was still raging, but Peter had
his focus back, and with his eyes on Jesus, he could
once again do the impossible. Peter would have
many other failures and victories in the days ahead.
And though he never walked on water again, he
was powerfully used by God.

Maybe you feel that you are sinking right now.
You're filled with fear, worry, and defeat. You
might be in the grip of some addiction. Maybe
your marriage is in trouble. Follow Peter's example
and cry out, "Lord, save me!" Jesus won't rebuke
anyone who is trying to come to Him by faith.
Besides, it's safer to be with Jesus in rough waters

than it is to be without Him in the boat. Just call out to Him, and He will lift you up again.

Mark's Gospel offers a fascinating detail about this story:

> Then He saw them straining at rowing, for the wind was against them. Now about the fourth watch of the night He came to them, walking on the sea, and would have passed them by. (Mark 6:48)

It was as though the Lord was waiting for their invitation. And later, when He was with the disciples on the road to Emmaus, we are told, "Then they drew near to the village where they were going, and He indicated that He would have gone farther" (Luke 24:28).

If you want Jesus to intervene in your life as you face storms, you can be assured that He will. Jesus is saying, "Come." But you need to say, "Lord, save me!" And He will. Just as He reached out and took hold of Peter, Jesus will reach out and take hold of you.

BREAKFAST WITH
JESUS

John 6: 22–71

B y 7:00 p.m. on October 20, 1968, only a few thousand spectators remained in the Olympic stadium in Mexico City. It was almost dark, and the last of the marathon runners were stumbling across the finish line. Finally, the spectators heard the wail of sirens from the police cars. As eyes turned to the gate, a lone runner, wearing the colors of Tanzania, staggered into the stadium. His name was John Stephen Akhwari, and he was the last of the seventy-four competitors. With a badly cut knee and a dislocated joint sustained from a fall earlier in the race, he hobbled the final lap around the track. The spectators rose and applauded as though he were the winner of the race. Afterward, someone asked him why he had kept running. He replied, "My country did not send me seven thousand miles away to start the race. They sent me seven thousand miles to finish it."

The Bible often compares the Christian life to running a race. The apostle Paul spoke of it on several occasions. Toward the end of his life, he concluded, "I have fought the good fight, I have finished the race, I have kept the faith" (2 Tim. 4:7). As he bid farewell to the believers from Ephesus, he said, "But none of these things move me; nor do I count my life dear to myself, so that I may finish my race with joy … " (Acts 20:24). And to the believers at Corinth, he posed this challenge:

> Do you not know that those who run in a race all run, but one receives the prize? Run in such a way that you may obtain it. And everyone who competes for the prize is temperate in all things. Now they do it to obtain a perishable crown, but we for an imperishable crown. (1 Cor. 9:24–25)

So the goal of a believer should not be simply to start the race, but to finish it. I've written a book on this vital topic called *Losers and Winners, Saints and Sinners: How to Finish Strong in the Spiritual Race* that you ought to read if you want to know more about how to be winner in the race of life.

And in the story we're about to read, we will see a great number of people who claimed to be followers of Jesus turn their backs on Him one day.

They simply left Him en masse. We will see why. And we will also learn about the relative handful of Jesus' followers who did not desert Him that day and discover what it was that kept them going. We'll find out what will keep us going as well, and why we should never, never quit.

There is a time to pray and a time to move.

Perhaps you will even see yourself in this story. Have you ever read a passage from the Bible that just didn't seem to make any sense? Has there ever been a time in your life when it seemed as though God didn't come through for you? Were you ever tempted to just give up trying to follow Jesus? If so, then you're in good company. You have a good idea of how Jesus' disciples most likely felt one day when Jesus laid down some of His most difficult teachings yet.

Although these truths were too hard for many, they were not too hard for the true believers. Instead of this being a day in which they gave up on their faith, they deepened it instead. This was a day when the wheat was separated from the chaff, when the true disciples were separated from the false ones. It was a day in which Jesus intentionally thinned out the ranks.

Notice how the story begins:

> On the following day, when the people who were standing on the other side of the sea saw that there was no other boat there, except that one which His disciples had entered, and that Jesus had not entered the boat with His disciples, but His disciples had gone away alone—however, other boats came from Tiberias, near the place where they ate bread after the Lord had given thanks—when the people therefore saw that Jesus was not there, nor His disciples, they also got into boats and came to Capernaum, seeking Jesus. And when they found Him on the other side of the sea, they said to Him, "Rabbi, when did You come here?" (John 6:22–25)

After His miracle of the Feeding of the Five Thousand (probably more like ten thousand, counting women and children), Jesus became exceedingly popular. In fact, His popularity had reached a fever pitch at this point—so much so that they wanted to take Him by force and make Him king. So Jesus told His disciples to leave immediately. As I pointed out in the previous chapter, a huge storm formed on the Sea of Galilee, causing the disciples to panic. But Jesus came to them on the water and joined them in the ship, and they were immediately at their destination (see v. 21). I don't know whether that means time flew quickly once Jesus was on board, or whether the boat literally zipped to the other side of the Sea of Galilee at lightning speed. I think it was probably the latter.

Meanwhile, back on the other side, morning had come, and the stomachs of the well-fed multitudes began to growl. There were no restaurants to go to and no vendors selling bread from carts as there would have been in Jerusalem. There were no fishermen bringing in the catch of the day. So the people thought to themselves, "Where's Jesus this morning?" Realizing He was gone, they went searching for Him and found Him on the other side: "Rabbi, when did You come here?" (v. 25).

They asked Him *when* He had come, and He responded by telling them *why* they had come: "Most assuredly, I say to you, you seek Me, not because you saw the signs, but because you ate of the loaves and were filled" (v. 26).

Jesus had compassion on them the day before, but now they fully reveal all they really care about, which is filling their growling stomachs. I can understand this, because there is nothing wrong with being hungry. God has given us certain physical drives in life, including a hunger drive, a thirst drive, and a sex drive, all of which are not evil or wrong when fulfilled in their proper place. For example, we should not live to eat, but eat to live. Sex is blessed of God in marriage, but not anywhere else. There is a time and a place for everything.

If God were small enough
to understand, He wouldn't be
big enough to worship.

The problem here was that these people were standing in the presence of God Almighty, the very Bread of Life, and all they could think about was breakfast.

It reminds me of the time when Jesus visited the home of Martha and Mary. While Mary sat at the feet of Jesus, the Bible tells us that "Martha was distracted with much serving" (Luke 10:40). She complained to Jesus, "Lord, do You not care that my sister has left me to serve alone? Therefore tell her to help me" (v. 41). Certainly there is a time to cook a wonderful meal and wash the dishes, and there is a time to sit and visit with close friends. In the same way, there is a time to work, and there is a time to worship. There is a time to pray, and a time to move.

And, there is a time to have breakfast and a time to wait on God—a lesson that this multitude had not yet learned. So Jesus used this opportunity to remind them of what a person's priority in life should be: "But you shouldn't be so concerned about perishable things like food. Spend your energy seeking the eternal life that I, the Son of Man, can give you. For God the Father has sent me for that very purpose" (John 6:27 NLT). Jesus was saying there is more to life than simply filling your stomach. On another occasion, Jesus told His disciples,

> "So don't worry about having enough food or drink or clothing. Why be like the pagans who are so deeply concerned about these things? Your heavenly Father already knows all your needs, and he will give you all you need from day to day if you live for him and make the Kingdom of God your primary

concern." (Matt. 6:31–33 NLT)

Jesus did not say, "Don't concern yourself with food and clothing or plan ahead for your needs." In fact, the Bible criticizes a person who is lazy and lives off the generosity of others instead of working for a living. What Jesus was saying was not to worry about having enough food and clothing, and not to make these things the driving force of their lives. We are not to merely seek success, power, possessions, or happiness. Instead, as we seek God first and foremost in our lives, everything we need will be provided for us. Job had the right idea when he said, "I have treasured the words of His mouth more than my necessary food" (Job 23:12).

We do not need to live in fear of spiritually falling away.

David Myers, professor of psychology at Hope College, spent six years examining hundreds of studies on happiness and concluded that once you get past the poverty, money doesn't help, no matter how much you buy: "The stockpiles of CDs, the closets full of clothes, the big screen stereo TV systems … clearly that doesn't do it. People having achieved that level of wealth have now adapted to it, and it takes new increments, a faster computer, a bigger TV screen, or whatever to 'rejuice the joy' that the initial purchase gained for them."[1]

So we don't need to look to material things for fulfillment. As Philippians 4:19 reminds us, "And my God shall supply all your need according to His riches in glory by Christ Jesus."

I find it interesting that although Jesus did not provide breakfast for these self-seeking people who came to Him for the wrong reasons, He would later serve breakfast to His disciples after they had been fishing all night:

> When they got there, they saw that a charcoal fire was burning and fish were frying over it, and there was bread. … "Now come and have some breakfast!" Jesus said. And no one dared ask him if he really was the Lord because they were sure of it. Then Jesus served them the bread and the fish. (John 21:9–13 NLT)

What is especially amazing to me about this story is the fact that only days earlier, this same Jesus had been tortured and crucified for the salvation of those who would believe in Him— which of course included these very men. No doubt those hands that had prepared this tasty breakfast still had large wounds in them. Yet it reminds us that God not only cared about the forgiveness of their sins, but He wanted them to be well-fed and taken care of.

Yet Jesus took a different approach with this fickle crowd. Their stomachs probably growled louder and louder as the morning grew longer. Maybe they thought, "Is He done with the sermon yet? We want breakfast!" So they thought they would help things along: "Therefore they said to Him, 'What sign will You perform then, that we may see it and believe You? What work will You do? Our fathers ate the manna in the desert; as it is written, 'He gave them bread from heaven to eat' " (John 6:30–31).

It was when they did understand Him that they went elsewhere.

Only yesterday, Jesus had performed a dramatic miracle for them, so impressive that they wanted to crown Him as their king right then and there. Yet here they were, needing to be convinced all over again. Jesus had rebuked the Pharisees and Sadducees, who also had tried to manipulate

Him into performing a miracle: "A wicked and adulterous generation seeks after a sign, and no sign shall be given to it except the sign of the prophet Jonah" (Matt. 16:4).

Maybe they should have taken a more straightforward approach: "Why don't you do that bread and fish miracle again? Better yet, why not show us how to do it, and we won't bother you anymore!" They had completely missed what Jesus said and went back to focusing on their stomachs. The Bible says, "But the natural man does not receive the things of the Spirit of God, for they are foolishness to him; nor can he know them, because they are spiritually discerned" (1 Cor. 2:14). They couldn't get food off their minds, even going so far as to mention manna. It was as if to say, "The fish and loaf thing yesterday was great. But why don't you give us manna today?" Manna, of course, was the mysterious food that God fed the Israelites. Each morning, they would find it on the ground outside their tents. But they soon tired of it, eating it for breakfast, lunch, and dinner. They had tried all of Moses' recipes from the cookbook, *Moses' 101 Recipes for Manna*. There were manna pancakes, manna malts, bamanna splits, and of course, everyone's favorite, mannacotti. Scripture tells us that manna had a sweet, almost honey-like taste to it. So maybe the crowd was looking for dessert.

At this point, Jesus pulled no punches and got really direct with them. He explained to them four very important things about conversion:

> But I said to you that you have seen Me and yet do not believe. All that the Father gives Me will come to Me, and the one who comes to Me I will by no means cast out. For I have come down from heaven, not to do My own will, but the will of Him who sent Me. This is the will of the Father who sent Me, that of all He has given Me I should lose nothing, but should raise it up at the last day. (John 6:36–39)

These people were no doubt impressed with Jesus. After all, they had wanted to make Him king. But they wanted it on their terms, not His.

NOT ALL WHO SEE WILL COME

So the first thing we learn about conversion from this story is that not all who see will come. Jesus said to them, "You have seen Me and yet do not believe" (v. 36). This crowd wanted a king who would heal them when they were sick, who would conform to their plans and goals, and who would cater to their wants and whims. And a lot of people still feel that way about Jesus today. They want Him as their short-order cook—their parachute in case of an emergency.

The reaction of this hungry multitude indicates that a person can have a certain amount of spiritual insight, yet not necessarily see enough. We can, as the apostle Paul said in Acts 26:18, have our eyes opened. But we still must turn "from darkness to light and from the power of Satan to the power of God."

ALL WHO ARE CHOSEN WILL COME

Second, we learn that all who are chosen will come. "All that the Father gives Me will come to Me," Jesus said (v. 37). This raises the question as to whether God chooses some and not others. In a sense, the answer is yes. That is not to say that God wants anyone to perish. Rather, He wants everyone to come to repentance (see 2 Peter 3:9). But does He simply choose or reject people at random? That certainly doesn't seem to be the case. Perhaps God's choice is based on the foreknowledge of who would choose Him.

So how do you know if you are chosen? Commit your life to Jesus Christ, and you will confirm that you are. Reject Him, and you will confirm that you are not. If you think this is too hard to grasp, that you cannot reconcile it in your mind, then welcome to the club. If God were small enough to understand, He wouldn't be big enough to worship.

ALL WHO COME ARE WELCOMED AND ARE SAFE FOREVER

Third, we see that all who come are welcomed: "The one who comes to Me I will by no means cast out" (v. 37). No matter what sins you have committed, God will welcome and forgive you. There are no exceptions. God graciously offers His forgiveness to all who come to Him.

God is not so much interested in quantity as He is in quality.

Fourth, all who come are safe forever. Jesus said, "Of all He has given Me I should lose nothing" (v. 39). And in John 10:28 He said, "I give them eternal life, and they shall never perish; neither shall anyone snatch them out of My hand." We do not need to live in fear of spiritually falling away. No one who has ever fallen away has done so against his or her will. Those who fall away make a series of choices that lead to spiritually destructive (and sometimes physically destructive) results.

Then Jesus said something that could almost sound bizarre, but would be understood by someone who was spiritual:

> "I am the living bread which came down from heaven. If anyone eats of this bread, he will live forever; and the bread that I shall give is My flesh, which I shall give for the life of the world." The Jews therefore quarreled among themselves, saying, "How can this Man give us His flesh to eat?" (John 6:51–52)

People often missed the point of Jesus' words, because they put too much of a literal interpretation on symbols He often employed. When He said, "Destroy this temple, and in three days I will raise it up" (John 2:19), they immediately thought He was talking about the massive Jewish temple in Jerusalem. But Jesus was speaking of the temple of His body. And when He said to Nicodemus, "Unless one is born again, he cannot see the kingdom of God" (John 3:3), the puzzled religious leader asked, "How can a man be born when he is old? Can he enter a second time into his mother's womb and be born?"

So when Jesus said, "I am the living bread which came down from heaven …" this was a hard one for His followers—and it still is. John tells us that "many of His disciples, when they heard this, said, 'This is a hard saying; who can understand it?' " (v. 60). A "hard saying" does not mean that Jesus' teachings are hard to understand, because really they are not. In reality, they sometimes are hard to keep. As long as these fair-weather followers could not fully understand Him, they hung around and asked questions. It was when they *did* understand Him that they went elsewhere. They left, because what they heard was so contrary to their own views.

There were three things Jesus said that this group had a hard time swallowing. And many people still have a hard time with these things today.

THE REALITY OF THE INCARNATION

The first was the teaching of the Incarnation. Jesus told them He was the True Bread that came down from heaven (see vv. 33, 38, 51). This implies that He had existed before His physical birth and was God's unique and only Son. At Christmas we celebrate the birth of Jesus. But the Incarnation tells us that Jesus was God who had come in the flesh, because there is no other way for us to know God apart from Him. This is one truth that seems more difficult than ever for people to accept: that Jesus Christ is the only way to God. But you cannot truly be a Christian and *not* believe this.

In our culture of moral relativism, this really rubs a lot of people the wrong way. After all, it seems too narrow, so dogmatic, and so intolerant. But in reality, it is simply believing what Jesus Christ plainly said: "I am the way, the truth, and the life. No one comes to the Father except through Me" (John 14:6). The Bible clearly teaches "there is one God and one Mediator between God and men, the Man Christ Jesus" (1 Timothy 2:5), and that "there is salvation in no one else! There is no other name in all of heaven for people to call on to save them" (Acts 4:12 NLT).

THE IMMINENT CRUCIFIXION

The second difficult thing Jesus said was that He needed to go to the cross:

> "I am the living bread which came down
> from heaven. If anyone eats of this bread, he
> will live forever; and the bread that I shall

give is My flesh, which I shall give for the life of the world." (John 6:51)

When Mel Gibson's *The Passion of the Christ* was released in 2004, a centuries-old debate broke out yet again: Who killed Jesus? Clearly, no one took His life. He willingly went to the cross for us. The cross is offensive, repulsive, and shocking—but necessary. As 1 Corinthians 1:23–24 tells us, "But we preach Christ crucified, to the Jews a stumbling block and to the Greeks foolishness, but to those who are called, both Jews and Greeks, Christ the power of God and the wisdom of God."

Clearly Jesus made this series of statements to intentionally thin out the ranks. That almost seems strange, but it really isn't. Jesus wanted to rid himself of fair-weather followers who really weren't followers at all. It reminds us that God is not so much interested in *quantity* as He is in *quality*. Are you a true disciple of Jesus or merely a fair-weather follower? Will you finish your race with joy or give up if it makes you unpopular or when things get a little tough?

John tells us that at this point, some who started the race with Jesus decided it was time to drop out of it: "From that time many of His disciples went back and walked with Him no more. Then Jesus said to the twelve, "Do you also want to go away?" (vv. 66–67).

It comes down to this. When we first come to Jesus, it's all about our needs. We don't wake up one morning and say, "I need to glorify God and seek His will!" Instead, it's more like, "Why is my life so empty and meaningless? What happens when I die?" So we come to Jesus. We discover prayer, a process whereby we can talk with and hear from God. Initially, we pray for what we want and need in life. We come to church and want to learn all we can and be as blessed as possible. And there is nothing wrong with any of that.

But as we grow and mature spiritually, we start making some discoveries. One is that it really is all about glorifying and seeking God. When we seek to be holy, we find that we are happy—not from seeking happiness, but from seeking God. We discover that prayer is not about what we want, but about what God wants. We find that developing and using the gifts God has given us is a blessing at church. It is not that we don't need to keep learning and growing, but we also need to be serving and giving.

A. B. Simpson wrote:

Once it was the blessing, now it is the Lord.
Once it was the feeling, now it is His Word.
Once His gifts I wanted, now the Giver alone.
Once I sought His healing, now Himself alone.[2]

Many have never come to this point. They are still in only a receiving, not giving, mode. They often become hypercritical and start taking things for granted. At the end of a church service in which many people have made decisions for Christ, they are the ones who are annoyed that the service ran four minutes late. They may think, "Well, I've learned all I can here. This church is no longer meeting my needs. I need a new church now." A person who thinks this way is one who needs to learn how to serve, how to mature, how to feed himself or herself, and how to be a disciple and a discipler of others.

People haven't changed much in two thousand years, have they? *We know you are the Bread of Life, Jesus, but we want breakfast!* But there were true followers of Jesus back then, just as there are today. Among them was Peter, who spoke up for himself and the others. They wanted Jesus to know they would not quit:

But Simon Peter answered Him, "Lord, to whom shall we go? You have the words of eternal life. Also we have come to believe and know that You are the Christ, the Son of the living God." Jesus answered them, "Did I not choose you, the twelve, and one of you is a devil?" He spoke of Judas Iscariot, the son of Simon, for it was he who would betray Him, being one of the twelve. (vv. 68–71)

And that is the mark of the true believer: he or she cannot quit. Peter first says, in effect, "Lord, we have been thinking about it. We have investigated the alternatives. We don't understand You at times. What You say does not always makes sense at the time. Others have laughed at us for following You. But we have looked at the alternatives, and it comes down to this: we have never found anyone who can do what You do. Where else would we go? No one speaks like You do and no one understands life like you do. That holds us."

Peter and those for whom he spoke up were one of three, distinct groups of disciples we find in this passage:

1. Those who won't quit, who can't quit, because their hearts have been captured. May this tribe grow, and may you be one of them.

2. Those who start out well, who follow Jesus for awhile, and then drop out and quit. If that describes you, then you need to get back into the race. You need to return to the Lord and seek Him.

3. Those who are Judases. They appear to be Christians, but they are not. They are connivers, deceivers, and liars. And to be quite frank, they are on their way to hell.

Which group do you find yourself in today? Are you a true disciple who cannot quit? Then I want to encourage you to run this race with endurance, "looking unto Jesus, the author and finisher of our faith" (Heb. 12:2).

That is the mark of the true believer: he or she cannot quit.

Are you someone who started running well, but dropped out of the race along the way? If you have been chasing after happiness, success, and fulfillment in life and keep coming up empty, remember that Jesus said, "I am the bread of life. He who comes to Me shall never hunger, and he who believes in Me shall never thirst" (John 6:35).

You can still return to the race and finish well.

And if you find yourself in the third category, then I want you to know that your eyes can be opened to the truth, but you must act upon it. Remember, Jesus said, "The one who comes to Me I will by no means cast out" (v. 37). It isn't too late to enter the race. So why not do so today?

ALONE WITH
JESUS

John 8: 1–11

A Florida newspaper ran a news item about a hungry thief who grabbed some sausages in a meat market, only to discover they were part of a forty-five-foot-long string. Tripping over them, he was hindered in his getaway, and the police found him collapsed in a tangle of fresh sausages. He was literally caught in the act (and in the sausage too).

Have you ever been caught in the act of doing something wrong? One of the central figures in the passage we're about to explore is a woman who wa caught in the actual act of adultery. Under the Law of Moses, she could have been put to death by stoning (see Lev. 20:10). But fortunately for her, she didn't get what she deserved, because she was brought before Jesus. And what could have been the worst (and potentially the last) day of her life turned out to be the best as she was transformed by her encounter with Christ. The same could be true for you as well.

Before we find out what Jesus did for this woman, let's look at the events leading up to it. John 7 closes with, "And everyone went to his own house" (v. 53), while John 8 opens with, "But Jesus went to the Mount of Olives." There is a stirring poignancy to those words. The Savior of the world, God in human form, was huddled under an olive tree, sleeping alone on a cold October night on the Mount of Olives. He had no home to return to, but instead went to commune with His Father. He clearly left us an example to follow. There are many times in which we need to get away from the crowd and spend time in communion with our Heavenly Father, because it is during those times that we find the resources to deal with the pressures that life can bring.

While Jesus was communing with heaven, they were communing with hell.

The Pharisees had probably been awake that night, hatching their scheme. While Jesus was communing with heaven, they were communing with hell. Whether to arrest Jesus was an easy decision, but how to pull it off was the problem. So some lawyer devised an apparent foolproof plan:

Now early in the morning He came again
into the temple, and all the people came
to Him; and He sat down and taught them.
Then the scribes and Pharisees brought to
Him a woman caught in adultery. And when
they had set her in the midst, they said to
Him, "Teacher, this woman was caught in
adultery, in the very act. Now Moses, in
the law, commanded us that such should
be stoned. But what do You say?" This
they said, testing Him, that they might
have something of which to accuse Him.
But Jesus stooped down and wrote on the
ground with His finger, as though He did
not hear. (vv. 1–6)

As we will see, sometimes even fool proof plans
can fail. And much to their surprise, Jesus turned
the tables on them:

So when they continued asking Him, He
raised Himself up and said to them, "He
who is without sin among you, let him throw
a stone at her first." And again He stooped
down and wrote on the ground. Then those
who heard it, being convicted by their
conscience, went out one by one, beginning
with the oldest even to the last. And Jesus
was left alone, and the woman standing in
the midst. (vv. 7–9)

The scribes and Pharisees may have looked holy, spouting Scripture in front of Jesus. But let's not make the mistake of thinking that everyone who quotes the Bible is necessarily a true believer. Those who quote Scripture to heartlessly condemn others are frequently the guiltiest of all. Those who are quick to find fault with others usually have greater fault in their own lives. This is precisely what Jesus was speaking of when He used the analogy of finding a speck in your brother's eye when you have a log in your own (see Matt. 7:3).

The sin that stands out here is not that of a woman who was unrighteous and knew it. The sin that stands out is that of the self-righteous who did not know it. If we know of someone who is falling in the area of sexual immorality, we should confront and restore them, not condemn them. Yes, this woman who had been caught in the very act of adultery had clearly failed. But what was worse was that these men had no compassion for her.

Galatians 6:1 offers the appropriate response if we know someone who has fallen into sin: "Brethren, if a man is overtaken in any trespass, you who are spiritual restore such a one in a spirit of gentleness, considering yourself lest you also be tempted." However, the way some people act, you would think this verse actually says, "Brothers, if a man is overtaken in any trespass, you who are spiritual condemn him, and then make sure you tell as many people as you can what he has done." The objective is to *restore*, not *destroy*, considering ourselves, lest we are tempted.

Why should we first consider ourselves? Because it could be one of us that needs restoration someday. We all have the potential to fall—and to fall big. There is not a single one of the Ten Commandments that each of us could not break, given the right set of circumstances. That is why Hebrews 2:1 warns us, "So we must listen very carefully to the truth we have heard, or we may drift away from it" (NLT). Part of the reason for Peter's denial of Jesus after His arrest was his refusal to believe Jesus' words.

Sadly, most of us know at least one person who has fallen into adultery, perhaps even more. Imagine the shock of the young pastor who heard a well-known evangelist say, "I have spent some of the happiest moments of my life in the arms of another man's wife. … " Then the evangelist added with a wink of the eye, "And that woman was my mother."

The young pastor thought, "That is so funny,

I just have to use that!" So a few weeks later as he was speaking to his congregation, the phrase came to him. "I have spent some of the happiest moments of my life in the arms of another man's wife," he said. But then his mind went blank and he couldn't remember the punch line. So after a long pause, he muttered sheepishly, "But for the life of me, I can't remember who she was!"

However, the real issue of adultery is no laughing matter. Countless marriages and lives have been destroyed by it, because adultery goes beyond the mere sexual act. It almost always includes deception and betrayal.

I received a heartbreaking letter from a man who had fallen into this sin. He attended Harvest Christian Fellowship for a time, and once was active in ministry. John (not his real name) told me in his letter:

> As you know, I'm sure, Mary [not her real name] and I are no longer husband and wife. Our marriage ended in divorce. ... Bottom line, Greg, I took my eyes off of God and placed them on circumstances surrounding me. Pride, lust, and the Enemy had their way. Before long, Mary (God's gift to me) no longer satisfied me and I committed adultery. In fact, the very night

that act took place, you and I crossed paths at the mall. I was there in a restaurant sitting with a coworker that I introduced as "Cindy." Remember? When I look back on that night, I'm reminded of when Judas came to Jesus in the Garden with the band of soldiers to arrest Jesus. And before he [Judas] identified Christ with a kiss, Jesus said to him, "Friend, why have you come?" In that moment Jesus was giving to Judas one more opportunity to turn to him. Greg, you were that person God used to cross my path that evening to wake me up, to warn me, "Don't do this!" I didn't listen. Needless to say, that decision and those to follow would systematically destroy my life. … I had lost everything: my relationship with God, my marriage, my reputation. Everything was gone. To look back on my life and see the destruction that has been done through selfishness, because I failed to take God seriously at His word … I virtually destroyed what life I had at the time. Even worse, I destroyed Mary's life as well.

John went on to describe in his letter the extent of the destruction his wrong decision produced.

God forgave John, but he paid a heavy price. My heart goes out to him, to Mary, and to any others who have gone down this sad road. Yes, God forgives, but there is still a "reaping of what has been sown" that follows.

SIX REASONS YOU SHOULD NEVER COMMIT ADULTERY

I am pleading with you: do not even consider this sin. Here are six reasons why.

First, you do incredible damage to your spouse. As the apostle Paul wrote in 1 Corinthians 6:16, you violate your oneness with your spouse by entering into this bond with another person: "And don't you know that if a man joins himself to a prostitute, he becomes one body with her? For the Scriptures say, 'The two are united into one' " (NLT). This is why Jesus gave a release clause from marriage, due to the seriousness of this offense. If, by God's grace, your spouse can find it in his or her heart to forgive you, the factor of trust is practically destroyed. That is because in most cases of adultery, it usually isn't a one-time occurrence. It is a practice that has required habitual deception and lying. And that is often as devastating as the act itself.

Second, you do incredible damage to yourself. If you commit adultery, then you have been in a backslidden state and have been rationalizing it for so long that you have probably lost any capacity for sound judgment. When you commit adultery, you have become vulnerable to this sin, and the Enemy will no doubt attempt to continue attacking you in this area. You will have crossed a line that can never be uncrossed. Will God forgive you? Yes. But others won't as quickly. And sadly, some never will. Radical measures will have to be taken to prevent it from happening again, because it will be a lot easier the second time than it was the first.

———◦◦◦———

It could be one of us that needs restoration someday.

———◦◦◦———

And if you think that it's as simple as divorcing your spouse and marrying the person you had been unfaithful with, think again. The problem is that in the new relationship, there always will be underlying suspicion, especially as marital tensions grow, that you will opt out and try your luck again with another partner. After all, you committed adultery with your previous spouse, so what would prevent you from doing it again? Second marriages are twice as likely as first marriages to end in divorce. That is not to mention the very real risk of contracting a sexually transmitted disease or HIV/AIDS.

Third, you do incredible damage to your children. If you have children, your own hand undermines your position as a spiritual leader in the home. Their trust in you is eroded, and as with your spouse, it will take years to regain. They may even in turn repeat your sin. Remember, David's own children did. David committed adultery with Bathsheba, and his son Amnon raped his own half-sister Tamar. David had Uriah killed, while Absalom killed his brother Amnon.

Fourth, you do damage to the church. The Bible tells us that "if one member suffers, all the members suffer with it; or if one member is honored, all the members rejoice with it" (1 Cor. 12:26). We are all interconnected as believers, and the victories and defeats of individuals affect the body as a whole. It was for this very reason that Paul exhorted the believers in Corinth to remove the immoral man from their midst, because "a little leaven leavens the whole lump" (1 Cor. 5:6).

Fifth, you do great damage to your witness and the cause of Christ. I need only to cite the damage of so-called televangelists to make my point. As the

prophet Nathan said to David after his adultery
with Bathsheba, "By this deed you have given great
occasion to the enemies of the Lord to blaspheme"
(2 Sam. 12:14).

Sixth, you sin against the Lord. This should
be the primary reason you would want to avoid
this sin. Joseph had the correct motive when he
rejected the advances of Potiphar's wife and told
her, "How then can I do this great wickedness, and
sin against God?" (Gen. 39:9). Sadly, this reason is
usually last on the list for many people.

SINS OF THE SPIRIT

So here was this woman, caught in the very act of
adultery. But these scribes and Pharisees could
care less about her. They wanted to trap Jesus.
Their sin was worse than hers, because theirs was a
sin of the spirit.

You see, sin is not always obvious. Of course,
some sins are, like murder, adultery, and
stealing. But others are not as apparent, like
pride, selfishness, and gossip. Sometimes we sin
in ignorance or presumption. That is why David
prayed, "Who can understand his errors? Cleanse
me from secret faults. Keep back Your servant

also from presumptuous sins; let them not have dominion over me. Then I shall be blameless, and I shall be innocent of great transgression" (Ps. 19:12–13).

There are both sins of the flesh as well as sins of the spirit.

According to Scripture, the sins of the heart can separate us from God just as easily as the sins of the body—and sometimes in a more destructive way because we are not aware of them. There are both sins of the flesh as well as sins of the spirit, as 2 Corinthians 7:1 tells us: "Because we have these promises, dear friends, let us cleanse ourselves from everything that can defile our body or spirit. And let us work toward complete purity because we fear God" (NLT).

A sin of the spirit is to go against what we know is true. Jesus made this distinction regarding the sin of the high priest, Caiaphas. To Pilate, Jesus said, "You could have no power at all against Me unless it had been given you from above. Therefore the one who delivered Me to you has the greater sin" (John 19:11). Jesus was referring to

Caiaphas or possibly Judas. Both of them knew the innocence of Jesus. Both deliberately did what they knew was wrong. When we have been schooled in the Scripture like Caiaphas or have been exposed to the truth and power of God like Judas, we are essentially without excuse. It is to knowingly sin against the light.

THE TRAP IS SET

Back to our story. Jesus knew exactly what was going on. He was not fooled by circumstances or appearances. They knew that Jesus was speaking to an early morning congregation in the temple. So they threw this woman down before Jesus, thinking they had Him for sure. They baited their trap and waited for Jesus to make His first mistake.

> *You will have crossed a line*
> *that can never be uncrossed.*

It really was something of a dilemma when you stop and think about it. If Jesus had said, "Stone her!" the people would have withdrawn from His just, but distant, touch. On the other hand, if He had said, "Let her go," He would be defying the

Law, and in effect saying, "Disregard the Law. Live as you please."

Sometimes people falsely interpret God's loving patience and willingness to forgive as leniency, a soft touch, or even approval. They don't realize it is "through the Lord's mercies we are not consumed, because His compassions fail not" (Lam. 3:22) and that "the Lord is not slack concerning His promise, as some count slackness, but is longsuffering toward us, not willing that any should perish but that all should come to repentance" (2 Peter 3:9). Some play with sexual sin today and seem to be getting away with it. They don't get caught—at least not right away. Nothing horrible happens, so rather than thanking God and stopping while they can, they do it again. But soon, the tell-tale signs begin to surface. A husband or wife gets suspicious. Others find out, and their reputation as a believer is destroyed, not to mention the ever-present guilt they carry every day. They hope the inevitable will not happen. They hope they will be the sole exception to the verse that says, "Be sure your sin will find you out" (Num. 32:23). But it will. Sooner or later.

It did with Samson. Although he had repeated warnings, he saw them as some kind of joke and kept pushing the envelope, so to speak. But let's not confuse God's mercy with God's leniency. As Ecclesiastes 8:11 warns, "When a crime is not punished, people feel it is safe to do wrong" (NLT).

> *A sin of the spirit is to go against what we know is true.*

THE TABLES ARE TURNED

The scribes and Pharisees were about to have their sin exposed. Jesus turned the white heat of His wrath on their sin instead of the woman's. John tells us, "But Jesus stooped down and wrote on the ground with His finger, as though He did not hear" (8:6). This is not the first time Scripture mentions God's writing. The Ten Commandments were written by the finger of God (see Ex. 31:18). When Belshazzar mocked God, he saw the writing of the same hand on the palace wall (see Dan. 5:5). Now we find the great Lawgiver turning the spotlight of the law on those who were so quick to quote it. It was as though Jesus was saying, "All right boys. You like to quote the law to condemn another? Let's see how you fare under its searching light."

The question of what He wrote on the ground is something the greatest minds of the church have grappled with for years. Perhaps Jesus wrote the Ten Commandments of the Law. They were originally written by the finger of God, so now God's finger was writing them again. Or maybe Jesus reminded them of His statement, "You have heard that it was said to those of old, 'You shall not commit adultery.' But I say to you that whoever looks at a woman to lust for her has already committed adultery with her in his heart" (Matt. 5:27–28). Then again, maybe Jesus wrote down the secrets of their lives. Many people have a secret sin they hope never will be uncovered. Even in the church, some live double lives, appearing to be something they really are not. Needless to say, they aren't fooling Jesus. Psalm 44:21 reminds us, "For He knows the secrets of the heart." And Romans 2:16 tells us that "God will judge the secrets of men by Jesus Christ."

Those who were oldest would have had the most sins to confess. John tells us that each one left, from the oldest to the youngest (8:9). The very Law these religious leaders were so quick to quote had driven them away from—and this woman to—Jesus. And that is exactly what the Law does. The Bible tells us, "So the law was put in charge to lead us to Christ that we might be justified by faith" (Gal. 3:24 NIV). The law can neither save nor change us. All it does is condemn us and send us to Jesus, who can both forgive and justify us. According to Colossians 2:13–14, "God made you alive with Christ. He forgave us all our sins, having canceled the written code, with its regulations, that was against us and that stood opposed to us; he took it away, nailing it to the cross" (NIV).

A NEW LEASE ON LIFE

One has to wonder what this woman must have been thinking at this point. At first, Jesus bewildered her. Then she sensed that Jesus was more concerned with the sin and hypocrisy of her accusers, and then with the accusation they had brought against her. Perhaps she looked up to see a flawlessness, a righteousness in His eyes, and at the same time, mercy and genuine compassion. Maybe her heart began to soften, and the rebellion, anger, and denial began to drain out of her.

She was left alone with Jesus, and He pierced the silence with a word she had not heard in a

long time, if ever: "Woman. ... " In the Greek
language, this was a term of respect used toward a
wife, a mother, a lady. It was the same word Jesus
used when He spoke to His own mother from the
cross. Whenever Jesus used this term, it spoke of
great tenderness.

Let's not confuse God's mercy
with God's leniency.

"Neither do I condemn you ... " He continued
(v. 11). How this must have shocked this
undoubtedly hardened woman. Like the woman at
the well, she probably had been used and abused
by men all her life. And the very men who quite
possibly had helped to condemn her soul had now
demanded her execution. In reality, she was still
immoral. She had been caught in the act. But the
reason Jesus could say, "Neither do I condemn you"
was that, in a short time, He would personally take
upon himself that very condemnation on the cross
of Calvary.

Notice He did not say, "Go and sin no more, and
as a result, I will not condemn you." This is very
important, because if that were the case, who could
escape condemnation? Thankfully, that is not what

Jesus said. Rather, He said, "Neither do I condemn you; [now, as a result of that recognition,] go and sin no more." We don't seek to live godly lives to win or find God's approval. We realize we have God's approval because of Jesus, so we live godly lives. The goodness of God leads us to repentance, as Romans 2:4 reminds us. As followers of Jesus, we are not bound by rules and regulations. Rather, we are constrained by His love. Paul said, "For the love of Christ constrains us … " (2 Cor. 5:14).

"Go and sin no more," Jesus told her. His act of forgiveness was followed by a challenge. He didn't just tell her she was forgiven and to be on her way. He also included this challenge. Implicit in His statement was a warning: "Don't keep living in this lifestyle." And He says the same to us as well: "Leave this lifestyle of sin!" This doesn't mean that God expects perfection, because we will fail. There is a difference between being sinless and wanting to sin *less*.

Did this woman believe? Did she begin a new life of sinning less? I think her response to Jesus' question, "Where are those accusers of yours? Has no one condemned you?" indicates that she did.

"No one, *Lord*," she told Him (v. 11). It very

well could be those words had never left her lips before. When the convicting power of God's Holy Spirit drove her accusers away, the woman came closer. Just one look into His eyes answered all her questions, melted all her doubts, and drove away all her fears. Jesus saw, in that moment, in a flash, that belief had occurred in her once-hardened heart.

The Lord did not condemn her; nor does He condemn us.

That is how belief can take place—in a flash, in a moment. We often assume that when we see someone walking forward during the invitation at a church service or an evangelistic event that, at that moment, he or she is becoming a believer. But the actual event of belief may have occurred much earlier. One statement may have brought it about, just a sudden realization of God's love washing over someone, like it happened with the thief on the cross. One moment, he was mocking Jesus, while the next moment, He was trusting in Him for his salvation.

Having forgiven this woman, Jesus then promised her three things.

Promise one: Her sins could be forgotten. Notice that He never mentioned her past. A good definition of justification is "just as if it never happened." When we are justified through faith in Jesus Christ, it's as though our sins never happened. God promises, "For I will forgive their iniquity, and their sin I will remember no more" (Jer. 31:34).

Promise two: She did not need to fear judgment day. The Lord did not condemn her; nor does He condemn us. As Romans 8:1–2 states: "There is therefore now no condemnation to those who are in Christ Jesus, who do not walk according to the flesh, but according to the Spirit. For the law of the Spirit of life in Christ Jesus has made me free from the law of sin and death."

Promise three: She had new power to face her problems. "Go and sin no more," Jesus told her. If you have been recently caught in the act of your own sin, or perhaps haven't been caught yet but have been playing around with it, then you need to come to Christ as fast as you can. Turn from your sin, and you will hear Him say, "Neither do I condemn you; go and sin no more."

Jesus didn't leave this woman in her sin. Yes, she had fallen down. But He helped her to get up again. And He will do the same for you.

BELIEVING IS
SEEING

John 9

When I came to faith in Jesus Christ, it was a pretty dramatic conversion. I wasn't raised in a Christian home. So I literally went from darkness to light overnight and changed my lifestyle and my friends as well. I hung around with a group of guys who had no interest in the things of God and were pretty surprised when they heard that I had become a Christian. In fact, I had one friend that I had known since elementary school. His name was also Gregg, and he couldn't believe it when I told him I had accepted Christ. He said, "Laurie, promise me you will not become one of these Jesus freaks, one of these religious fanatics. Promise me you won't carry a Bible around and wear a cross around your neck and say, 'Praise the Lord.' "

I said, "Gregg, I promise you I will never do that. You know me. You know I am not that kind of a person. I will never carry a Bible around. I will never say, 'Praise the Lord.' I am going to kind of do a modified version of this, sort of my own version."

Two weeks passed before I saw Gregg again. Now a lot can happen in two weeks when you have given your life to Christ. I started going to Calvary Chapel of Costa Mesa and listening to Pastor Chuck Smith teach the Word of God. And it was transforming my life day by day. He had said that we needed to go out and start telling others about Jesus, so I thought, "Well, I have almost two weeks under my belt. I'd better get out and do my part."

He saw Jesus. And that is why he saw everything else in its proper perspective.

So I was in Newport Beach, out telling people about Jesus, when I saw Gregg walking toward me. He looked at me and I looked at him, and suddenly we both realized what had happened. There I stood with a cross around my neck that someone had given me. I was carrying a Bible. And before I could catch myself, the first statement out of my mouth was, "Praise the Lord!" He laughed. And I laughed. I said, "I know how this looks, Gregg. You think I have lost my mind. But I am telling you that

Christ has changed my life and it is wonderful." He actually was listening to me, and I thought, "Well, maybe Gregg will come to the Lord."

As I was telling him about what had been taking place in my life over the past two weeks, some guy was eavesdropping on our conversation. He suddenly interrupted me and said, "I have a few questions for you, Christian." *Who was this guy and where did he come from?* I thought to myself.

I said, "Excuse me, but I am just talking to my friend here."

"Yeah, but I have a few questions for you about God." I had been a Christian for the whole of two weeks, but I felt I could handle whatever he asked me. So he started firing off question after question, and I had no idea what to say.

Then Gregg joined in. "Yeah, Laurie, what about that?"

I said, "I don't know." I don't remember exactly what that guy asked me, but I do remember being dumbfounded. I went home feeling pretty defeated that day. I prayed, "God, I am sorry for not knowing." And I determined to study the Bible so I would be able to have some answers for a situation like that.

EASY TO ASK, HARD TO ANSWER

Most of us have found ourselves in the scenario I just described. We either have been asked those questions or wondered about them ourselves. They are questions like, "Why is there suffering in the world?" or "What about the person who has never heard the gospel? Will that person be condemned to hell?" You might be surprised to know that these questions are not necessarily new. Many of them date all the way back to the time of Christ. Here in John 9, we will see many of those questions raised.

Before us is the story of a blind man who was healed by Jesus, and he became a believer as a result. We have all heard people say, "Seeing is believing." But in this man's case, it was, "Believing is seeing." He saw things he never before had seen. He saw not just the faces of friends and family for the first time. He saw not just the beauty of God's creation all around him. He saw spiritually as well. He saw what the purpose of life was and what really mattered. Best of all, He saw Jesus. And that is why he saw everything else in its proper perspective.

However, before any of this took place, the first question was raised:

> Now as *Jesus* passed by, He saw a man who
> was blind from birth. And His disciples
> asked Him, saying, "Rabbi, who sinned, this
> man or his parents, that he was born blind?"
> Jesus answered, "Neither this man nor his
> parents sinned, but that the works of God
> should be revealed in him. (vv. 1–3)

If this man was blind from birth, then how
could his sin cause his blindness? It seemed like
a tactless question on the part of the disciples.
But some of the Jews believed in a version of
reincarnation, that is, that the soul moves from
body to body. The status of each successive body,
whether human or animal, was the direct result
of the quality of life the soul led in the previous
body. Thus, a good life would result in rebirth to a
higher-quality form, while a "bad" life would result
in rebirth to a lower-quality form. Many believe in
this same kind of idea today as they embrace the
teachings of the law of karma, which is a central
foundation of Hinduism and other Eastern-rooted
philosophies. Karma teaches that good deeds
are rewarded and bad deeds are punished. In
fact, sixty percent of Americans believe that
reincarnation is possible. In contrast, the Bible
teaches that we do not preexist in some state

before this life. Rather, we become living souls at conception, as Psalm 139 indicates:

> For You formed my inward parts; You covered me in my mother's womb. I will praise You, for I am fearfully and wonderfully made; marvelous are Your works, and that my soul knows very well. … Your eyes saw my substance, being yet unformed. And in Your book they all were written, the days fashioned for me, when as yet there were none of them. (vv. 13–14, 16)

Jeremiah spoke of God knowing him in his mother's womb (see Jer. 1:5). We have but one life to live on this earth, and in this life we determine where we will spend eternity. But beyond the grave, there are no other opportunities to do so. According to Hebrews 9:27, "It is destined that each person dies only once and after that comes judgment" (NLT).

The disciples' curiosity brings us to the often-asked question of why God allows suffering. Why does He allow babies to be born with disabilities? Why does He allow war, terrorism, illness, and tragedy?

BLAMING GOD

Many have turned against God because of a tragedy that occurred in their lives. Among them is CNN founder Ted Turner. As a young boy, he was deeply religious and intended to become a missionary. But his younger sister was diagnosed with lupus, and despite young Ted's fervent prayers, she died. He described how she would run around in pain, begging God to let her die. "My family broke apart," he said. "I thought, 'How could God let my sister suffer so much?' " Turner has described himself as an atheist or agnostic and once said that "Christianity is a religion for losers."[1] Turner could not reconcile the concept of a loving God coexisting with human suffering.

Maybe you, too, feel as though you were dealt a harsh hand in the game of life. Perhaps your parents divorced, a loved one died unexpectedly, or you have a disability or know someone who does. You ask, "Why?" Our human intellects and notions of fairness reject the apparent contradiction between a loving God and a world of pain. In the classic statement of the problem, either God is all-powerful, but not all-good, and therefore doesn't stop evil. Or, He is all-good, but not all-powerful, and therefore cannot stop evil. The general tendency is to blame God for evil and suffering and to pass all responsibility for it on to Him.

WHAT DID WE DO TO DESERVE THIS?

What the disciples were getting at on this day was, "Can our physical suffering on Earth be the result of sin?" Jesus' answer was, "Neither this man nor his parents sinned … " (v. 3), meaning in this case, there was no correlation between the man's condition and sin. However, Jesus did not say, "You've got it all wrong. Suffering is just a random event that has nothing to do with sin." Jesus addressed only the specifics of this particular case.

In a broad sense, sickness, disabilities, and even death are all the result of sin. We must remember that man was not created evil, but perfect, innocent, exempt from aging, immortal, and with the ability to choose right or wrong. Our first parents made that choice, and they chose wrong. Had Adam and Eve never sinned, then the curse of sin would not have come as a result: "Therefore, just as through one man sin entered the world, and death through sin, and thus death spread to all men, because all sinned" (Rom. 5:12). The thing we must keep in mind is that it is humanity, not God, who is responsible for sin.

———————

The Bible teaches that we do not preexist in some state before this life.

———————

Some might ask why God didn't create Adam and Eve in such a way that it was impossible for them to sin. The reason is that God has given us a free will to choose good or evil and right or wrong. It seems that it would be a much better (and certainly safer) world if God did not allow us to exercise our free will. In many ways, free will is both our greatest blessing and our worst curse. But if God had not given us free will, then we would be mere robots that are pre-programmed in our choices and actions. Instead, God wants to be loved and obeyed by creatures who voluntarily choose to do so. Love is not genuine if there is no other option.

In the weeks and months following 9/11, the one question I was asked most often was, "Why did God allow this?" Some even went as far as to say the attacks were God's judgment on the United States. But I disagree. In Luke 13, Jesus told a story about a tower that fell on a group of Gentiles. He asked the rhetorical question, "Were they the worst sinners in Jerusalem? No, and I tell you again that unless you repent, you will also perish" (Luke 13:4–5 NLT).

AN INDISPUTABLE FACT

Jesus was addressing the fact that people die. Period. He was saying, in essence, "You had better be careful, because you might die too. You are a sinner as well. It could happen to you." The point was that those who died were not any worse than anyone else. It could happen to anyone. No one is exempt. Everyone dies. There are no exceptions.

This does not mean that God is unfair, however. It doesn't mean that when someone dies, it was God's judgment. It just means that individual's time to leave this earth came. And it will come to everyone. As Hebrews 9:27 says, "It is appointed for men to die once, but after this the judgment." Some die young, some die old, some die slowly, and some die quickly. But everyone dies. We just have a hard time accepting that fact. We even shy away from the word by substituting phrases such as "passed away," "passed on," or "no longer with us."

Even insurance salesmen avoid using the "d-word" in their sales pitch and instead say things like, "If something should happen to you. … " Our use of these very terms emphasizes the fact that we are basically afraid of death. It baffles, bothers, and frightens us. But why? Because we are afraid to die. The Bible speaks of "those who have lived all their lives as slaves to the fear of dying" (Heb. 2:15 NLT). It is our classic fear of the unknown.

In this life we determine where we will spend eternity.

But if you are Christian, then you have hope. Yes, there are things in life that don't make sense. Good things happen to bad people. And bad things happen to good people. But we need to remember that when a Christian suffers, God will always, in some way, use it or be glorified through it. He may sometimes even remove the suffering. However, when an unbeliever suffers, there is no great purpose in it whatsoever. When a Christian dies, he or she will go immediately into the presence of God. That is an unchangeable truth. And it is a great hope and comfort to all believers.

THREE THINGS WE SHOULD KNOW ABOUT SUFFERING

Sometimes we can see God's hand in suffering, while at other times we cannot. But I would suggest that you consider three ways suffering can work in your life.

One, suffering can have a corrective influence on us. In other words, it is the idea that God will allow or send some pain into our lives to get our attention.

It is humanity, not God, who is responsible for sin.

I had the opportunity to be a guest on the *Larry King Live* program in August 2005. Larry raised the question of why God allowed suffering, and I responded, "You know, Larry, I had a lady come into our office Sunday morning after the church service, and she has breast cancer. And it was that suffering that got her attention to get her to come back to church and to start seeking a spiritual life and getting right with God. And I think of the psalmist who writes, 'Before I was afflicted, I went astray. But now I have kept your word.' And C. S. Lewis said, 'God whispers to us in our pleasures … but He shouts to us in our pain.'[2] Pain is God's megaphone."[3]

Larry interrupted, "How do you know it's not a crutch? I mean, 'I've got breast cancer. I've got to pray something.' You know—every believer in the foxhole."

I responded, "Thank God for that crutch, Larry, He's not a crutch to me, He's a whole hospital."

Larry chuckled and told his producer that was a good line and he should write that down. But I was only describing how God can use suffering in our lives to get our attention.

When Jesus healed the paralytic man at Bethesda, He said, "See, you have been made well. Sin no more, lest a worse thing come upon you" (John 5:14). So yes, sickness can come as a result of our own sin, but that very sickness can bring us to Jesus, as it did with this man. Many come to Christ because of an unexpected illness, tragedy, the death of a loved one, or a personal crisis such as a divorce or an addiction to drugs or alcohol.

God can also use these things to correct His wayward children. As David said, "Your rod and Your staff, they comfort me" (Ps. 23:4). To me, it is a great comfort to know that God loves me enough to correct me. It proves that I am His very child. After all, we can't correct someone else's child, but we can and should correct our own. We read in Hebrews 12:

> And have you entirely forgotten the encouraging words God spoke to you, his children? He said, "My child, don't ignore it when the Lord disciplines you, and don't be discouraged when he corrects you. For the Lord disciplines those he loves, and he punishes those he accepts as his children. ... " No discipline is enjoyable while it is happening—it is painful! But afterward there will be a quiet harvest of right living for those who are trained in this way. (vv. 5–6, 11 NLT)

For example, maybe a Christian is deliberately going astray and goes out drinking and partying, only to get pulled over and charged with a DUI. Or maybe a wayward believer is rebelling against God and suddenly gets sick or loses her job. God may be using His megaphone to speak to the one who has become deaf to His voice. That is what happened to Jonah. God sent a storm to get his attention. So when sickness, suffering, tragedy, or hardship comes our way, we should be asking, "Lord, are you trying to tell me something? Because if you are,

I'm all ears!" Having caught your attention, the Lord may indeed remove the suffering. Or, it could be there for another reason, which leads us to the second way God works through our suffering.

Free will is both our greatest blessing and our worst curse.

Two, suffering can be constructive in our lives. This is when God allows suffering to produce a desired result. As 2 Corinthians 4:17–18 reminds us,

> For our present troubles are quite small and won't last very long. Yet they produce for us an immeasurably great glory that will last forever! So we don't look at the troubles we can see right now; rather, we look forward to what we have not yet seen. For the troubles we see will soon be over, but the joys to come will last forever. (NLT)

Paul spoke of his physical suffering as his "thorn in the flesh":

> But to keep me from getting puffed up, I was given a thorn in my flesh, a messenger from Satan to torment me and keep me from getting proud. Three different times I begged the Lord to take it away. Each time he said, "My gracious favor is all you need.

My power works best in your weakness." So now I am glad to boast about my weaknesses, so that the power of Christ may work through me. (2 Cor. 12:7–9 NLT)

When a Christian suffers, God will always, in some way, use it or be glorified through it.

Sometimes we ask the Lord to take something away, and He says, "No, I am going to work through it." That is what He did with Paul. So what Paul was experiencing was *constructive* suffering.

Three, our suffering can be used to glorify God. Our life experiences can be used to help others. Sometimes when you go through hardship, you can bring a special measure of comfort to someone else who is going through something similar. And God, in His amazing knowledge, can cause all things to "work together for good to those who love God, to those who are the called according to His purpose" (Rom. 8:28). We have seen this in the life of believers like Joni Eareckson Tada, Corrie ten Boom, and many others. There are also times when God will glorify himself by removing the suffering. And that is what He was doing in the life of the blind man here in John 9. Jesus answered, "Neither this man nor his parents sinned, but that the works of God should be revealed in him. I must work the works of Him who sent Me while it is day; the night is coming when no one can work" (vv. 3–4).

IS HEALING REALLY POSSIBLE?

Instead of dealing with how this man ended up blind, Jesus was saying that He would glorify himself through it. He would heal this man. And God is still healing people today. Isaiah speaks of this promise of Jesus' healing: "But He was wounded for our transgressions, He was bruised for our iniquities; the chastisement for our peace was upon Him, and by His stripes we are healed" (53:5). Peter, commenting on this verse, wrote, "Who Himself bore our sins in His own body on the tree, that we, having died to sins, might live for righteousness—by whose stripes you were healed" (1 Peter 2:24). The word "healed" Peter used is a verb that always speaks of physical healing in the New Testament and is always used in connection with physical ailments. So it is clear that God can heal us if it is within His will. So why are some of us still sick? I think one reason may be a simple lack of asking. James tells us, "You do not have because you do not ask" (4:2).

> *No one is exempt. Everyone dies. There are no exceptions.*

However, in the case of this blind man, Jesus chose to do a miracle in his life. But He did it in a rather unorthodox manner:

> Then he spit on the ground, made mud with the saliva, and smoothed the mud over the blind man's eyes. He told him, "Go and wash in the pool of Siloam" (Siloam means Sent). So the man went and washed, and came back seeing! (vv. 6–7 NLT)

Think of all the ways Jesus healed people. Some would touch Him, like the woman who touched the hem of His garment. He would speak to some, and they would be healed. And some He would touch. In this man's case, He spit in the dirt, wiped it on his eyes, and told him to go wash. What a strange sight this man must have been as he hurried through the streets of Jerusalem, dirt mixed with saliva caked on his eyes. When he reached the pool of Siloam, he must have counted the steps as he descended, then washed the dirt from his eyes.

And for the first time in his life, he could see.

Imagine what he must have felt at that moment. Who did this for him? Why? Would he ever see Him again? But he didn't have much time to contemplate these questions or even to enjoy his newfound sight, because it wasn't long before he was called before the religious authorities and cross-examined:

> Now as it happened, Jesus had healed the man on a Sabbath. The Pharisees asked the man all about it. So he told them, "He smoothed the mud over my eyes, and when it was washed away, I could see!" Some of the Pharisees said, "This man Jesus is not from God, for he is working on the Sabbath." Others said, "But how could an ordinary sinner do such miraculous signs?" So there was a deep division of opinion among them. Then the Pharisees once again questioned the man who had been blind and demanded, "This man who opened your eyes—who do you say he is?" The man replied, "I think he must be a prophet." (9:14–17 NLT)

This man didn't know if he would ever see Jesus again. How easily he could have downplayed the truth. He knew these Pharisees were angry. He would not want to provoke them and risk being barred from worship, essentially being ostracized. The entire lives of the Jewish people revolved around the local synagogue, including their personal, business, and social lives. But this man simply could not deny what had happened to him. Jesus had opened his eyes.

THE COST OF FOLLOWING CHRIST

This serves as a reminder that when we choose to make a real stand for Jesus, it will cost us. Friendships can end and tensions can increase, because people will know you are changed. Do those around you know which side you are on? Have you ever made a public profession of your faith in Jesus Christ? Though it is true it will cost you to follow Jesus, it is also true that it will cost you more *not* to follow Him.

Meanwhile, these religious leaders could not let this go:

> So for the second time they called in the man who had been blind and told him, "Give glory to God by telling the truth, because we know Jesus is a sinner." "I don't know whether he is a sinner," the man replied. "But I know this: I was blind, and now I can see!" "But what did he do?" they

asked. "How did he heal you?" "Look!" the man exclaimed. "I told you once. Didn't you listen? Why do you want to hear it again? Do you want to become his disciples, too?" Then they cursed him and said, "You are his disciple, but we are disciples of Moses. We know God spoke to Moses, but as for this man, we don't know anything about him." (vv. 24–28 NLT)

You may not have the answers to everyone's questions. But you just may know more than you think. Often you will not discover that until you are "under the gun," so to speak.

Let's put ourselves in this man's sandals for a moment. One day, he is completely blind. He had never seen a blue sky, a cloud, or a sunset. He had never laid his eyes on the face of another person or knew what water, mountains, or trees looked like. Then one day, seemingly out of nowhere, this stranger named Jesus comes along and opens up the entire world of sight to him. Upon receiving this precious gift, he is of course overjoyed and elated. Yet all these Pharisees could do was argue about the things that didn't matter.

The same thing happens to us when we come to Christ. Our world is changed overnight. The weight of sin is gone. The guilt in our hearts is replaced by peace. Yet people want to argue with us. They want us to explain the problem of suffering or the problem with this or that.

WHAT RELIGION CAN'T DO, JESUS CAN

But I like the response of this man in our story: "I know this: I was blind, and now I can see!" (v. 25). Jesus would now do even more for this man:

> When Jesus heard what had happened, he found the man and said, "Do you believe in the Son of Man?" The man answered, "Who is he, sir, because I would like to." "You have seen him," Jesus said, "and he is speaking to you!" "Yes, Lord," the man said, "I believe!" And he worshiped Jesus. Then Jesus told him, "I have come to judge the world. I have come to give sight to the blind and to show those who think they see that they are blind." The Pharisees who were standing there heard him and asked, "Are you saying we are blind?" "If you were blind, you wouldn't be guilty," Jesus replied. "But you remain guilty because you claim you can see."
> (vv. 35–41 NLT)

While religion turned this man away, Jesus took him in. Have you been disillusioned with religion?

Have you tried to keep all the rules and regulations, but still come up empty? Jesus is waiting for you with open arms, ready to open your eyes.

In telling the Pharisees, "If you were blind, you wouldn't be guilty," Jesus was saying, in essence, "You are responsible for the truth you know. If you were blind, then you would not be held accountable for truth you were unable to see. But if you, being Pharisees, claim that you can see, yet willfully ignore the truth of my Word, then you will be held accountable and guilty. You saw the light yet chose to live in darkness."

This addresses the question, "What about the person who has never heard the gospel? What about the people living a jungle somewhere who have never heard of Jesus? Are you Christians saying that a person won't go to heaven based solely upon where he or she lives?" According to the Bible, God doesn't work this way. God is perfectly holy and perfectly just. Therefore, it is against His nature to condemn someone who is ignorant of His truth. In fact, Scripture declares that God is loving, patient, and longing for fellowship (see 2 Peter 3:9). God will judge us according to the truth we have received. We will not be held accountable for what we do not know.

This, however, doesn't excuse us from all responsibility; otherwise we might claim that ignorance is bliss. No matter where we live on Earth, we as humans were born with eternity in our hearts (see Eccl. 3:11). Each of us was born with a soul—a sense that life should have meaning and purpose. But if we turn away from what little we know to be true, this shows we don't really want to know God. It isn't ignorance; it's rebellion. The truth is that we don't really want to change our lives.

God will always reveal himself to the one who really wants to know Him.

Romans 1:20 tells us that God places the knowledge of himself in our hearts: "From the time the world was created, people have seen the earth and sky and all that God made. They can clearly see his invisible qualities—his eternal power and divine nature. So they have no excuse whatsoever for not knowing God" (NLT).

I believe that if a person is a true seeker of God, then He will reveal himself to him or her. Jeremiah 29:13 promises, "And you will seek Me and find Me, when you search for Me with all your heart."

The Bible tells us about a man named Cornelius, who was very religious and was constantly praying to God. Cornelius had never heard of Jesus Christ, but he was asking God to reveal himself to him. God answered the prayers of Cornelius and sent Peter to preach the gospel to him. When Cornelius heard that wonderful message, he believed. That is because he was a true seeker. And God will always reveal himself to the one who really wants to know Him. We may have honest questions about God, and there is nothing wrong with that. It has been said that skepticism is the first step toward truth. But there is a big difference between skepticism and unbelief. Skepticism is open to believing, while unbelief is refusing to believe. Skepticism is honesty, while unbelief is stubbornness. Skepticism is looking for light, while unbelief is content with darkness.

There is a big difference between skepticism and unbelief.

An unbeliever has no intention of changing or believing. Unbelievers will offer up well-worn excuses and arguments, but the fact of the matter is that even when confronted with evidence to refute their unbelief, they reject it out of hand. That is because they do not want to believe. But knowledge brings responsibility.

Jesus put it this way:

> Their judgment is based on this fact: The light from heaven came into the world, but they loved the darkness more than the light, for their actions were evil. They hate the light because they want to sin in the darkness. They stay away from the light for fear their sins will be exposed and they will be punished. (John 3:19–20 NLT)

We need to pray that God would open the eyes of unbelievers, just as He opened the eyes of the blind man.

Perhaps something has happened in your life recently that has caught your attention. Maybe you have been going through a time of suffering. It might be *corrective* suffering to get your attention and put you on the right track again. Or it may be *constructive* suffering to achieve a desired effect in your life and make you more Christ-like. Or, God may allow it that He may be glorified in it. Whatever it may be, I would encourage you to turn your life over to Him, and in the words of Jesus, say, "Not as I will, but as You will" (Matt. 26:39).

And remember, you can tell people, especially unbelievers, how God has brought you through your trials. You can tell them that once you were blind, but now you see.

6 AN ABUNDANT LIFE

John 10:10–11

L ife. This is what I was searching for as a young man—not just existence, but life. My big question was not, "Is there life after death?" It was, "Is there life during life?" That is what we all want: a life that is worth living, a life that matters.

A story is told about Abraham Lincoln, who was surprised one day when a rough-looking man drew a revolver and thrust it in his face. Mr. Lincoln figured that a discussion or debate was out of the question at that point. So with all the calmness and confidence he could muster, Lincoln asked, "What seems to be the matter?"

The stranger replied, "Well, some years ago, I swore an oath that if I ever came across an uglier man than myself, I'd shoot him on the spot."

A wave of relief came over Lincoln. Then he said, "Shoot me. For if I am an uglier man than you, then I don't want to live!"

We all want a life that is worth living. We don't

want to merely exist. It has been said, "The tragedy of life is not that it ends so soon, but that we wait so long to begin it." How true that is.

LACKING LIFE

Many years ago, a young artist in Florence, Italy had labored long and hard over a marble statue of an angel. When he finished, he asked the master artist, Michelangelo, to examine it. No master looked over the work more carefully than Michelangelo. It appeared perfect in every way. The artist waited for Michelangelo's response. His heart nearly broke when he heard, "It lacks only one thing." But Michelangelo didn't tell him what it lacked. For days the young artist could not eat or sleep, until a friend called on Michelangelo and asked him what he thought. Michelangelo said, "It lacks only life."

That could be said of so many people today. They have all that one should supposedly have to be happy: a good job, a family, a house … but they lack life.

Most of us could say, at some point along the road of life, "If I had known what I know now, I would have lived differently. I would have done things differently so that I would have had a better life." Perhaps this statement from one ninety-year-old man says it best: "If I'd known I was going to live this long, I would have taken better care of myself."

We all want a life that is worth living.

We all want a better life. And in speaking of this, Jesus said, "The thief does not come except to steal, and to kill, and to destroy. I have come that they may have life, and that they may have it more abundantly" (John 10:10). The Bible often uses contrasts to make a point. Here, God shows us the consequences of both right and wrong choices. We see this in the examples of Cain and Abel as well as Abraham and Lot. Jesus spoke of a narrow road that leads to life and the broad road that leads to destruction (see Matt. 7:13). He also spoke of the wise man who built his house on the rock, and the foolish man who built his house on the sand (see Matt. 7:25–27).

THE ENEMY OF THE SHEEP

And here in John 10:10, we see both God's plan and Satan's plan. Satan's plan for your life is to steal, to kill, and to destroy. He wants to ruin your life. He would then seek to destroy and ultimately kill you. He accomplishes this through sin. And sin can be so alluring. But once the devil has his claws in you, he will pull you down so fast that you won't even know what hit you. Satan's end game is destruction, misery, and death. You may be familiar with *The Four Spiritual Laws*, a tract published by Campus Crusade for Christ International, which says that God loves us and has a wonderful plan for our lives.

Satan's end game is destruction, misery, and death.

Well, if the devil were ever to put his agenda in tract form, it would read, "Satan hates you and has a horrible plan for your life." Yes, it sounds shocking. But it's true. The devil is such a master at making evil look good and good look … well, lame, uncool, and out of fashion … evil.

The thief this verse is referring to is the enemy of sheep, such as a bear, lion, or wolf. The enemy's goal is to kill and eat the sheep. But in contrast to that wicked agenda is the plan of our Shepherd, Jesus. He wants us to "have life, and that … more abundantly." In the next verse, Jesus offers a description of himself as the *Good* Shepherd: "I am the good shepherd. The good shepherd gives His life for the sheep" (v. 11). The word "good" Jesus used here is full of meaning. Not only does it mean good as in morally good, but it also means, "beautiful, winsome, lovely, attractive." So Jesus is the beautiful, winsome, lovely, attractive Shepherd. And this Good Shepherd's primary objective for His flock is that they flourish, are well-fed and cared for, and are content and satisfied. He tells us as His followers, "Do not fear, little flock, for it is your Father's good pleasure to give you the kingdom" (Luke 12:32). And the kingdom of God, we are told in Romans 14:17, "Is righteousness and peace and joy in the Holy Spirit."

THE ABUNDANT LIFE DEFINED

So what exactly is the abundant life Jesus was speaking of? Let me first say what it *isn't*. The abundant life Jesus spoke of is not necessarily a *long* one. But it certainly is a *full* one. Breakthroughs in medical science can add years to our lives. But they cannot add life to our years. Nor is this abundant life one that is necessarily free from sorrow or sickness, although God certainly does spare us many sorrows that we might otherwise have had. And He often preserves us from sickness. No, this abundant life Jesus promises is not a state of constant euphoria. I find it interesting how some people think that Christians should have a permanent smile plastered across their faces. I've had people come up to me and say, "Greg, smile!!" Of course, the Christian life includes smiling, but not necessarily all the time.

The best way to describe the abundant life is a contented life.

Perhaps the best way to describe the abundant life is a *contented* life. This contentment comes from the knowledge that our Good Shepherd is capable of handling every emergency that will come our way. Our Good Shepherd is always looking out for our best interests, and it is His very joy to lead us to green pastures, beside still waters, and through the valley of the shadow of death. Our English word "abundance" comes from two Latin words, which mean "to rise in waves" and "to overflow." The translation of the first word conveys the image of the constant, crashing of waves on a shore. It is endless. Surfers will check the surf report to see where the best swell is, but one thing is sure: those waves will keep coming, over and over and over again. The translation of the second word suggests the idea of a flood overflowing a river, caused by heavy rains. When we put it all together, here is what we have: The abundant life is one in which we are content in the knowledge that God's grace is more than sufficient for our needs, that nothing can suppress it, and that God's favor for us is unending. The abundant life means unending, consistent contentment.

WHAT DOES IT TAKE?

Are you content? Are you happy with what you have and where you are right now? Or do you feel that if you were only a bit smarter, or better looking, or more successful, or had more money, *then* you would be content?

A wealthy employer once overheard one of his employees say, "If only I had one thousand dollars, then I would be perfectly content."

Knowing that his own money had never brought him any inner peace, he said to this employee, "Because I would like to see someone who is perfectly contented, I'm going to grant your desire." Then he gave her the money and walked away.

But before the employer was out of earshot, he

heard her remark almost bitterly, "Why on earth didn't I say $2,000?"

It is human nature to always want more. After experiencing many ups and downs in his life, Paul wrote,

> I have learned how to get along happily whether I have much or little. I know how to live on almost nothing or with everything. I have learned the secret of living in every situation, whether it is with a full stomach or empty, with plenty or little. For I can do everything with the help of Christ who gives me the strength I need. (Phil. 4:11–13 NLT)

Paul did not learn contentment from a theory in a classroom. He learned it in the school of life, the school of hard knocks. He had experienced pain and pleasure, health and sickness, weakness and strength, wealth and poverty, and being seen as a hero to some and as a villain to others.

Some people are like thermometers. They merely register what is around them. If the situation is tense and difficult, then they register tension and irritability. If the situation is stormy and uncertain, they register worry and fear. If the situation is calm, quiet, and comfortable, they register relaxation and peacefulness.

Other people, however, are like thermostats.

They regulate the environment. The way they act and react has a direct effect on others. In a sense, they control the atmosphere rather than allowing the atmosphere to control them.

Paul was like a thermostat. He wasn't angry when he was barely making ends meet. At the same time, he wasn't uneasy when God was supplying above and beyond what he needed. That is because his contentment wasn't based on *what* he had, but on *whom* he knew. Hebrews 13:5 exhorts us, "Let your conduct be without covetousness; be content with such things as you have. For He Himself has said, 'I will never leave you nor forsake you.' " It is because God has said, "I will never leave you nor forsake you" that we can be content.

LESSONS FROM A SHEPHERD

Let's look at another very familiar passage that brings this truth home, a picture of a Shepherd and His sheep:

> The Lord is my shepherd; I shall not want.
> He makes me to lie down in green pastures;
> He leads me beside the still waters. He
> restores my soul; He leads me in the paths
> of righteousness for His name's sake. Yea,
> though I walk through the valley of the
> shadow of death, I will fear no evil; for You

are with me; Your rod and Your staff, they comfort me. You prepare a table before me in the presence of my enemies; You anoint my head with oil; My cup runs over. Surely goodness and mercy shall follow me all the days of my life; and I will dwell in the house of the Lord forever. (Ps. 23)

David, a shepherd, penned these beloved words that have brought comfort to millions. As one who observed and understood sheep, it dawned on him one day that he was just like those sheep he faithfully watched over. He probably was sitting against a rock, with rod and staff nearby, watching his flock. After a nice meal of grass, they were satisfying their thirst as they drank from a cool, refreshing stream. It was a picture of total contentment: *The Lord is my shepherd; I shall not want.*

Here in this beloved psalm, we discover five things about living life to its fullest.

First, the sheep did not lack rest. The sheep were content and willing to eat and rest because they felt safe. Sheep can be very skittish. In his excellent book, *A Shepherd Looks at Psalm 23*, Philip Keller points out some traits about sheep, including the fact that they must be completely free of fear, hunger, and disturbances before they are willing to lie down.[1]

This psalm begins with contented sheep that are at rest. They have found their Shepherd to be good, one who is able to meet their needs and ensure their freedom from anxiety. However, it is important to remember that these things are available only to those who belong to the Good Shepherd. Only the person who has said, "The Lord is my Shepherd" can also say, "I shall not want."

Some people are like thermometers.

The sheep are at rest under the Good Shepherd. And having had a fine and filling meal, what is the next thing to do? Take a nap, of course! You know you are very comfortable around someone when you are willing to sleep in his or her presence. When you are asleep, you are vulnerable, and you can look (and sound) pretty silly. But with the Lord as our Shepherd, we are well-fed, content, comfortable, and secure.

There simply is no substitute for the knowledge that our Shepherd is near, because we live a most uncertain life. Any hour can bring disaster, danger, and distress. We never know what new trouble a day will bring, and it is often the unknown or unexpected that causes us the greatest anxiety. This is when we need to remember the Shepherd is near, as the psalmist reminds us: "I will both lie down in peace, and sleep; for You alone, O Lord, make me dwell in safety." And Psalm 121:4 promises, "Behold, He who keeps Israel shall neither slumber nor sleep." So take a nap. You are saved and safe. Not only that, but if the Lord is your Shepherd, you can lay your head on your pillow with a clean conscience.

They merely register what is around them.

The second thing we discover from this psalm about living life to the fullest is that *because the Lord is our Shepherd, we will have guidance in life:* "He leads me beside the still waters. … He leads me in the paths of righteousness for His name's sake" (vv. 2–3). Sheep need to be led. If left to themselves, they will wander off to dangerous places. Or due to the fact they are creatures of habit, they will never leave a place where they once found good grazing. Sheep have been known to completely destroy a pasture because they keep grazing until they've eaten every blade of grass and every root. In the same way, we so often will make the wrong decisions when left to ourselves. We hang out with the wrong people, go to the wrong places, and do the wrong things.

We, by nature, are all wanderers. Sometimes we follow the Good Shepherd, but other times we try to go in the wrong direction, and the Good Shepherd has to stand in our way to stop us. Have you ever had that happen? Balaam did. We find his story in Numbers 22. When Balaam was willing to accept payment for cursing the Israelites, God told him no. But Balaam decided to do it anyway, until his donkey talked some sense into him.

As Balaam was going the wrong direction, God sent an angel to stand in his way. Interestingly, the donkey saw the angel, but Balaam did not. The donkey bolted off the road and into a field. So Balaam beat it until it moved back onto the road again. This time, the road led between two walls, where the angel was waiting with sword drawn. The donkey tried to go around the angel, crushing Balaam's foot against the wall. So the angel went further down the road to a spot so narrow that the donkey could not get past at all. So the donkey simply collapsed.

By this time, Balaam was in a rage, beating the donkey again and again. So the Lord miraculously opened the donkey's mouth and it rebuked the disobedient prophet: "What have I done to you, that you have struck me these three times?" That is amazing—a donkey was talking. But even more amazing is the fact that Balaam responded without skipping a beat.

He said, "Because you have made me look like a fool! I wish there were a sword in my hand, for now I would kill you!"

"Am I not your donkey on which you have ridden, ever since I became yours, to this day? Was I ever disposed to do this to you?" asked the donkey.

> *It is because God has said,*
> *"I will never leave you nor forsake*
> *you" that we can be content.*

"No," Balaam admitted. And then God opened his eyes, and he saw the angel standing in the road with a drawn sword. At that point, Balaam fell facedown on the ground. Then the angel rebuked this stubborn prophet:

> "Why have you struck your donkey these three times? Behold, I have come out to stand against you, because *your* way is perverse before Me. The donkey saw Me and turned aside from Me these three times. If she had not turned aside from Me, surely I would also have killed you by now, and let her live." (Num. 22:32)

If you have been stopped in your tracks when you were trying to do the wrong thing, then rejoice. It is a reminder that God loves you.

Only the person who has said, "The Lord is my Shepherd" can also say, "I shall not want."

For some of us, it isn't that we want to go to the wrong place. It's that we don't want to go anywhere at all. We are fat, lazy, complacent sheep. So our Good Shepherd will periodically shake up our world and lead us on. It might be a move to start a new ministry. It might be a new business opportunity. But as followers of Jesus, it is important that we don't live in the past, but in the present, and that we keep moving forward toward the future.

The third thing we learn from this psalm is that *because He is our Good Shepherd, we will be safe*: "Yea, though I walk through the valley of the shadow of death, I will fear no evil; for You are with me … "(v. 4). This verse often has been quoted to offer words of comfort to those who are dying, and that is good. But this verse is primarily speaking of the Shepherd's ability to protect the sheep in moments of danger.

I find this illustrated clearly in a letter I received from a young man named Chris, who was on duty in Iraq. Chris, along with thousands of other young service men and women, lives daily in the "valley of the shadow of death":

> I am a staff sergeant in the Army National Guard out of Charlotte, North Carolina. I am a team chief for a fire support team, but we have been working with the Iraqi police for the time that we've been here. I have a wonderful, spirit-filled wife and three beautiful children. We have been here in Iraq since late February 2004 and we are scheduled to return home sometime in January. I can't tell you how excited I am to be coming home. I have such a greater appreciation for life and all the little things

we sometimes take for granted. It has been a difficult and dangerous year here, but by His grace we have been safe and successful. I was told this deployment could be my greatest test of faith ever and it has. My faith has been tested time and again, but I believe it has made me stronger and even more dependent on our God. …

Chris was praying for God's protection and trusted Him in the face of danger. God answered his prayers and protected him and now he has returned home.

The Good Shepherd will watch over you as well. When we belong to the Shepherd, we are indestructible until He determines our time here on Earth is done. Then we will go to heaven. So you see, it is a win-win proposition.

We would all prefer to live on a mountaintop rather than in "the valley of the shadow of death." We would like to be airlifted from peak to peak, from blessing to blessing. But the fact is that fruit does not grow on mountaintops, but in valleys.

Notice that David said, "Yea, though I *walk* through the valley … " (emphasis mine). Walking requires movement, which means that we need to keep moving in this Christian life. And remember, those valleys won't last forever.

Fourth, we discover that *because He is our Good Shepherd, we will have provision*: "You prepare a table before me in the presence of my enemies; You anoint my head with oil; My cup runs over" (v. 5). God will always provide for your needs, no matter what.

There simply is no substitute for the knowledge that our Shepherd is near.

My dog knows that I will feed him each and every day. So when he gets up in the morning, follows me down the stairs, and waits, he is content knowing that I will put his breakfast in his bowl. There are the familiar signs: the rustling of the bag, the sound of the food going into the bowl, and the extra food pellets on the floor. And if he whines, I tell him, "No!" Of course, dogs will always want "people food," but that can hurt, even kill, them. For example, chocolate is a favorite food among people, but it can kill a dog. And pet owners make a mistake if they give their dogs what they want instead of what they need.

God will give us what we need—not necessarily what we want—for our own good.

Fifth, we see that *because He is our Good*

Shepherd, He will guide us safely home to heaven:
"Surely goodness and mercy shall follow me all the
days of my life; and I will dwell in the house of
the Lord forever" (v. 6). As followers of the Good
Shepherd, we not only have life during life, but we
also have life after death. As I said, it's a win-win
proposition.

Of course, Satan's alternative is death during
life, and death for all eternity. His alternative is
the second death: "But the cowardly, unbelieving,
abominable, murderers, sexually immoral,
sorcerers, idolaters, and all liars shall have
their part in the lake which burns with fire and
brimstone, which is the second death" (Rev. 21:8).

Are you prepared for life after death? Are you
experiencing life during life? Are you content?
This can only happen when the Lord is your
Shepherd. Remember, Jesus said, "I am the good
shepherd. The good shepherd gives His life for the
sheep" (John 10:11).

Sheep need to be led.

Jesus died on the cross so we can have this
wonderful relationship with God. It's the kind of
relationship that brought a confused, young boy

like me to Christ at age seventeen. It's also the kind of relationship that sustained a soldier like Chris in Iraq. And it's the kind of relationship that will see you through this life and into the next.

RIGHT ON TIME

John 11

Has it ever seemed like God has let you down? Have you ever felt as though He didn't come through for you in your hour of need, that He forgot about you somehow, or that He simply was too late?

If you have ever felt this way, then you are in good company, because some of God's most choice servants have felt the same way.

We all live on schedules. We govern our lives by the clock, and we expect God to do the same. We go to work at a certain time and leave at a certain time. We go to bed and wake up at a certain time. We even live our lives for a certain amount of time. And we often spend too much time on the nonessentials, on things we wish we never had to do.

In an average lifetime, Americans will spend six months sitting at traffic lights waiting for them to change, one year searching through desk clutter looking for misplaced objects, eight months opening junk mail, two years attempting to call people who aren't in or whose line is busy, and five years waiting in line.[1] That is a lot of wasted time.

Of course, God isn't bound by our time zones. He lives in eternity. He has His own schedule, and He is never late. Ecclesiastes 3:11 tells us, "He has made everything beautiful in its time. … "

So let's look at a story that beautifully illustrates how something that can appear to be a mistake on God' part is actually part of His perfect plan for us. It is a story that shows us that God is always right on time—His time.

> Now a certain man was sick, Lazarus of Bethany, the town of Mary and her sister Martha. … Therefore the sisters sent to Him, saying, "Lord, behold, he whom You love is sick." When Jesus heard that, He said, "This sickness is not unto death, but for the glory of God, that the Son of God may be glorified through it." Now Jesus loved Martha and her sister and Lazarus. So, when He heard that he was sick, He stayed two more days in the place where He was. Then after this He said to the disciples, "Let us go to Judea again." (John 10:1–7)

Jesus loved Martha and her sister and Lazarus, who lived in the village of Bethany, not far from Jerusalem. Jesus spent a lot of time in their home, eating meals with them and enjoying their fellowship and friendship. Martha, Mary, and Lazarus really could say that Jesus was their personal friend.

His delays are to be interpreted in the light of His love—and not the other way around.

So when Lazarus grew seriously ill, they just knew that Jesus would heal him. They probably expected Him to drop whatever He was doing and rush to Bethany to help out His friend. So Martha and Mary sent a message to Jesus: "Lord, behold, he whom You love is sick" (v. 3).

In the original language, the word "love" used here speaks of friendship love. In other words, Mary and Martha were saying, "Lord, your friend is sick. Jesus, your buddy Lazarus needs your help right now."

Notice, however, that this was not an invitation or even a request. They didn't say, "Lord, please come immediately." They just assumed that because Lazarus was a personal friend of Jesus, then He would hurry there. However, they didn't tell Jesus what to do. They simply told Him that His friend was sick. They understood that He would know what to do. They assumed He would come and heal him or at least speak the word and Lazarus would be made better.

―――――

They wanted a healing.
But He wanted a resurrection.

―――――

Also notice the basis of their appeal. They said, "Lord, behold, he whom You love is sick." They did not say, "Lord, the one who *loves You is sick.*" Didn't Lazarus love Jesus? Absolutely. Did Mary and Martha love Him? Without a doubt. But they did not base their prayer on their worthiness or even their friendship. They didn't say, "Hey Lord, the one that loves You and is your good friend is sick." And that is something we should keep in mind. Don't appeal to God on the basis of your worthiness. Appeal to Him on the basis of His love for you.

WHEN WE DON'T UNDERSTAND

So, Jesus heard their request. And then He stayed two more days in the place where He was (vv. 5–6).

Immediately we think this is a contradiction. After all, if Jesus really loved Lazarus, why didn't He immediately go and heal him? When hardship, tragedy, or even death comes into our lives, we might ask the same. It is hard to see through eyes filled with tears.

Even though we cannot see how a situation will end or why it has happened to us, we can know that it flows through the love of God and is controlled by Him. Therefore, His delays are to be interpreted in the light of His love—and not the other way around.

Jesus wanted to do above and beyond what Martha, Mary, and Lazarus could imagine. They wanted a healing. But He wanted a resurrection. They thought only of friendship, but He thought of ultimate, sacrificial love. They thought only of temporal comfort, but He thought of eternal comfort.

Meanwhile, Lazarus was getting worse and worse. Then suddenly he died. He was gone. It was over, and Jesus was nowhere to be found. Then four days later, there He was, strolling into town after Lazarus was dead, buried, and in the process of decomposition.

Martha rushed out to meet Him, unable to contain her disappointment and hurt and pain. The

Bible tells us, "Now Martha said to Jesus, 'Lord, if You had been here, my brother would not have died. But even now I know that whatever You ask of God, God will give You" (vv. 20–21). Allow me to loosely paraphrase: "Lord, You blew it. We pinned our hopes on the fact that You would heal our brother, and You didn't even show up for the funeral. You missed everything."

Now in her defense, she still addressed Jesus as "Lord." She was still speaking to Him. She still acknowledged that He was in control: "If you had been here, my brother would not have died." She also added, "But even now I know that whatever You ask of God, God will give You," so there was still a measure of hope on her part.

There is nothing wrong with going to God and saying, "Lord, I love you, but I don't quite understand this. I don't quite know why you are letting this happen to me. I don't know why you haven't taken this away from me. Where were You?"

When something bad happens, we think, "How could this possibly be the will of God?" That is a difficult question, because we dwell only on this side of eternity. We don't see the big picture.

When God allows a tragedy, difficulty, or the

death of a loved one, there are some things we will never understand. Paul said, "For our light affliction, which is but for a moment, is working for us a far more exceeding and eternal weight of glory" (2 Cor. 4:17).

> *Jesus simply wanted to do more than Mary and Martha asked Him to.*

Jesus wanted to help Martha get an eternal perspective on her problems. Here is what it came down to: Jesus simply wanted to do more than Mary and Martha asked Him to. We must remember not to limit God in our prayers, recognizing that He is "able to do exceedingly abundantly above all that we ask or think, according to the power that works in us" (Eph. 3:20).

WHEN GOD WEPT

Now it's Mary's turn:

> Then, when Mary came where Jesus was, and saw Him, she fell down at His feet, saying to Him, "Lord, if You had been here, my brother would not have died." Therefore,

when Jesus saw her weeping, and the Jews
who came with her weeping, He groaned
in the spirit and was troubled. And He
said, "Where have you laid him?" They said
to Him, "Lord, come and see." Jesus wept.
Then the Jews said, "See how He loved him!"
(vv. 32–36)

Here we are given a glimpse into the utter
humanity of Jesus. We celebrate His deity—and
justly so. He is the Mighty God, the Everlasting
Father, and the Prince of Peace (see Isa. 9:6). But
He was also a man, and there are two indications of
that in these verses: He groaned and He wept.

First He groaned. The word used here for
"groaned" comes from an ancient Greek term that
describes a horse snorting. In the context, it speaks
of letting out an involuntary gasp. One translator
put it this way: "He gave way to such distress of
spirit, it made His body tremble." Have you ever
had one of those moments? It's a combination of
anger and sorrow.

The sorrow is understandable. But what was
He angry about? Was He angry with Martha? I
don't think so. Was He angry with Mary? Again,
I would say no. Was He angry with the people
nearby? Not necessarily. I think He was angry
with death. I think He was angry with the fact that

humanity has to go through something like this,
that we have to attend funerals for people we love,
that we have to say good-bye to them. This caused
Him anger.

His so-called delays are delays of love.

And then He wept. Weeping is not something
that we men generally feel comfortable doing. In
contrast, women are usually more willing to express
their emotions openly, while many guys tend to fight
it—maybe because of the perception that it isn't
manly to cry. But I have a two-word rebuttal for that:
Jesus wept. Who was more of a man than Jesus? He
was the manliest man who ever lived, and yet He
wept. It's the shortest verse in the Bible—and one of
the most powerful.

What prompted this sorrow from the Lord?
He saw Mary and the others weeping, and He
was touched. Jesus wept because He noticed their
weeping. He was moved by their sorrow.

In the same way, when He sees our tears, He
is touched. The Bible even says God puts our tears
into His bottle (see Ps. 56:8). If it touches us, it
touches Him. If it causes us pain, it causes Him pain.

Now what the Lord suggests next almost seems a
bit on the morbid side:

> Then Jesus, again groaning in Himself,
> came to the tomb. It was a cave, and a stone
> lay against it. Jesus said, "Take away the
> stone." Martha, the sister of him who was
> dead, said to Him, "Lord, by this time there
> is a stench, for he has been dead four days."
> (vv. 38–39)

Today when a person dies, he or she is usually embalmed. But in the first century, once a body was placed in a tomb, the process of decomposition was immediate. Four days had passed. So to say, "Lord, by this time there is a stench," was understating the fact.

The whole thing did seem a little insensitive, after all. In our day, it would be like saying, "Jesus, Lazarus is in the hospital. Could you come and visit him?" But He doesn't come to the hospital. He doesn't even show up for the funeral. Then He comes strolling in four days later and says, "OK, let's dig him up and open the coffin." That is what Jesus was essentially asking. What was the point of that? Yet there was something in Jesus' words that instilled confidence in everyone. And so they went and moved away that massive stone from Lazarus' tomb:

> And Jesus lifted up His eyes and said,
> "Father, I thank You that You have heard
> Me. And I know that You always hear Me,

but because of the people who are standing
by I said this, that they may believe that
You sent Me." Now when He had said these
things, He cried with a loud voice, "Lazarus,
come forth!" And he who had died came out
bound hand and foot with graveclothes, and
his face was wrapped with a cloth. Jesus said
to them, "Loose him, and let him go."
(vv. 41–44)

What a moment! "Lazarus, come forth!" Jesus
said. It is a good thing He called Lazarus by name,
because if Jesus had just said, "Come forth," every
body in every grave would have come out at once.
Here was Lazarus, bound in his graveclothes,
inching his way out of the tomb. No doubt, it was a
little difficult for Lazarus to get around. So Jesus
gave the command to undo his graveclothes. "Let
the guy out," He was saying. Jesus hadn't forgotten
Lazarus after all. He had a plan all along—a plan
that Martha, Mary, and the others just couldn't see
at the time.

WHEN GOD SEEMS LATE

So what can we learn from this story? First of
all, we learn that God is never late. His so-called
delays are delays of love. And God's silence can
even be a silence of love. He wants us to pour our

hearts out to Him. That is why it is never dangerous to pray, "Not my will, but Yours be done." It may not be until the very end of our lives that we will be able to see the Lord's wisdom and plan unfolding. Then again, it may not be until we are in eternity, looking into the very face of Jesus. Until then, we must trust Him and know that He wants to enter into our sorrows and into our pain and into our hurt.

The three Hebrew teenagers, Shadrach, Meshach, and Abed-Nego, could have been tempted to believe that God was late, that He had forgotten about them. The king had given a decree that all should bow before a golden image of himself—or die in a blazing furnace of fire. So when the theme music played, all the people obediently fell prostrate before the image—all the people except the three Hebrew boys, that is. The king was so enraged that he commanded the fire to be heated seven times hotter than it already was. They were given another chance to change their minds, but they would not. The heat from the fire was so intense that it killed the guards who had been assigned the unpleasant task of throwing Shadrach, Meshach, and Abed-Nego into it.

Why didn't the Lord come and scorch this idolatrous king and his followers? Where was He? God was waiting for Shadrach, Meshach, and Abed-

Nego *in* the furnace. And when they were thrown
in, much to the king's surprise, he saw four—not
three—figures walking around in the furnace: "
'Look!' he answered, 'I see four men loose, walking
in the midst of the fire; and they are not hurt, and
the form of the fourth is like the Son of God' "
(Dan. 3:25).

*Sometimes God delivers us
from the trial, and sometimes
He delivers us in it.*

Sometimes God delivers us *from* the trial,
and sometimes He delivers us *in it*. In the case of
Shadrach, Meshach, and Abed-Nego, God received
greater glory by allowing them to go through this
fiery trial instead of delivering them from it.

We also find this to be true when the children of
Israel crossed the Red Sea. Moses had demanded
the release of the Israelites time and time again,
but Pharaoh resisted, making their existence more
miserable than ever in Egypt. Finally, after God's
judgment came, Pharaoh relented and let the
people go. Joy filled their hearts as they began their
massive exodus out of Egypt and to the Promised

Land. But soon they realized a major obstacle was before them. It was called the Red Sea: "Then Moses stretched out his hand over the sea; and the Lord caused the sea to go back by a strong east wind all that night, and made the sea into dry land, and the waters were divided" (Ex. 14:21).

They were amazed as God caused the very waters of this mighty sea to part and hover on each side of them, forming mass, liquid walls. Things were looking good when, much to their horror, they looked behind them and saw the heavily armed Egyptian army coming after them in their chariots. As they got closer and closer, the Israelites thought all was lost. Then God came through:

> But early in the morning, the Lord looked down on the Egyptian army from the pillar of fire and cloud, and he threw them into confusion. Their chariot wheels began to come off, making their chariots impossible to drive. "Let's get out of here!" the Egyptians shouted. "The Lord is fighting for Israel against us!" (Ex. 14:24–25 NLT)

Then the waters closed back in, drowning the Egyptian army. But notice when God came though: "early in the morning" (v. 24). Another translation refers to this as "the morning watch" (NKJV), which is the fourth watch. So there it is again: the fourth watch—the same time of day when Jesus came to the disciples on the Sea of Galilee.

WHEN WILL HE COME AGAIN?

So you see, God is never late; He is always on time. And as we look at the world around us right now, we wonder how long it will be until the Lord returns. As we see horrible violence, perversion, and people not only breaking God's laws, but also flaunting their wicked lifestyles, we wonder, "When will He come again?"

Peter addressed this and assured us of God's perfect timing when he wrote:

> Knowing this first: that scoffers will come in the last days, walking according to their own lusts, and saying, "Where is the promise of His coming? For since the fathers fell asleep, all things continue as they were from the beginning of creation." … But, beloved, do not forget this one thing, that with the Lord one day is as a thousand years, and a thousand years as one day. The Lord is not slack concerning His promise, as some count slackness, but is longsuffering toward us.
> (2 Peter 3:3–4, 8–9)

Does it seem late to you right now? It does to me. Romans 13:12–14 tells us,

> The night is far spent, the day is at hand. Therefore let us cast off the works of darkness, and let us put on the armor of light. Let us walk properly, as in the day, not in revelry and drunkenness, not in lewdness and lust, not in strife and envy. But put on the Lord Jesus Christ, and make no provision for the flesh, to fulfill its lusts.

Or, as another translation puts it:

> The night is nearly over, the day has almost dawned. Let us therefore fling away the things that men do in the dark, let us arm ourselves for the fight of the day! Let us live cleanly, as in the daylight, not in the "delights" of getting drunk or playing with sex, nor yet in quarreling or jealousies. Let us be Christ's men from head to foot, and give no chances to the flesh to have its fling! (PHILLIPS)

God is never late;
He is always on time.

Yes, it is getting late. But He will not be late. He will be back right on time. Remember the fourth watch is that time just before the rising of the sun. He is coming again. And He will be right on time.

8   NO REGRETS

In the 1960s, at the zenith of The Beatles' popularity, John Lennon said, "Christianity will go. It will vanish and shrink. I needn't argue about that; I'm right and I will be proved right. We're more popular than Jesus now; I don't know which will go first—rock 'n roll or Christianity."[1]

Dear John: Who's more popular now?

The fact is that Jesus is more popular than ever. In January 2004, *The Tennessean* ran an article entitled, "The Popular Jesus Is Emerging," which said, "It can be debated whether or not America is a Christian nation. But one thing is certain, according to author Stephen Prothero: Everybody loves Jesus. And not just the usual suspects. In addition to Christians, America has Hindus, Jews, Buddhists and atheists who adore Jesus."[2] The article went on to say the fascination with Jesus was the subject of two classes at Vanderbilt University: "Jesus in Popular Culture" and "Jesus in Film." Prothero was quoted as saying, "I'm pretty comfortable saying that the United States is unique. The obsession with Jesus is unparalleled."

It is worth noting that every time we read about Mary in Scripture, she is at the feet of Jesus.

This is nothing new. Jesus was popular in the first century too, especially after He raised Lazarus from the dead. His name was on everyone's lips. Wherever He went, people thronged Him. The problem was, the same people who made Him popular soon turned on Him, because they never understood His real mission.

Even to His own, handpicked disciples, He was not fully understood. That is, until His crucifixion and resurrection from the dead. But there was one exception among His followers. It wasn't John, who was known for his spiritual perception. It wasn't Peter, James, Matthew, or Andrew. This person wasn't even one of the twelve disciples. In fact, it wasn't a man at all. It was a woman. She had greater spiritual insight than those who had spent every waking hour in Jesus' presence for nearly three years. Her name was Mary—the same Mary of Mary-and-Martha fame, the friend of Jesus, and the sister of Lazarus.

CHOOSING WISELY

It is worth noting that every time we read about Mary in Scripture, she is at the feet of Jesus. Perhaps that is why she had such insight. When the Lord came to visit her house, she wisely sat at His feet, even as Martha was slaving away in the kitchen. Jesus said to Martha, "You are worried and troubled about many things. But one thing is needed, and Mary has chosen that good part, which will not be taken away from her" (Luke 10:41–42).

Mary, no doubt led by the Holy Spirit, seemed to grasp a truth that was largely missed by the others: the fact that Jesus had to die. Not only did she have a unique understanding of who He was, but she also gave Him a wonderful gift. She gave Him the most precious thing she owned. For this, she not only was commended, but her gift was a memorial that would never be forgotten.

It's interesting to see which miracles, teachings, and events were recorded by the Holy Spirit through Matthew, Mark, Luke, and John. In his

Gospel, John wrote, "There are also many other things that Jesus did, which if they were written one by one, I suppose that even the world itself could not contain the books that would be written" (21:25).

We naturally would have gravitated toward the more dramatic miracles, or the great empires and leaders that coexisted with Jesus and the apostles in their day: the Caesars, the wonders of Rome, the great battles that were fought. But the Bible says very little about these things. Rome is presented merely as a backdrop for the most important story ever told. The great King Herod is a bit player. Caesar is briefly referenced.

God chose to record the event of which we are about to read to show us that He sees things differently than we do. Besides, the nations, their leaders, and their politics are but a drop in the bucket to Him (see Ps. 2:1–4).

So what great thing did Mary do? What was it that so impressed Jesus? It wasn't necessarily a practical thing, but it was a heartfelt one. Mary decided to seize the moment and once again sit at His feet. Then she offered her gift to Jesus:

Then, six days before the Passover, Jesus came to Bethany, where Lazarus was who had been dead, whom He had raised from the dead. There they made Him a supper; and Martha served, but Lazarus was one of those who sat at the table with Him. Then Mary took a pound of very costly oil of spikenard, anointed the feet of Jesus, and wiped His feet with her hair. And the house was filled with the fragrance of the oil. (John 12:1–4)

Mary had a perception that no one else seemed to have.

Things had been coming to a head in Jesus' ministry. There had been a number of increasingly confrontational exchanges between Jesus and the religious leaders. They wanted Him dead, plain and simple. But the problem was that Jerusalem was swarming with visitors for Passover. If they arrested Jesus, who was very popular among the people at this point, it could cause a riot.

Jesus was aware of all this, and He was looking forward to an evening with friends in Bethany. He and the disciples would be having dinner with Mary, Martha, and the newly resurrected Lazarus at the home of Simon the leper. I'm sure there must have been a lively conversation going on. Jesus had just delivered The Olivet Discourse, so there surely must have been questions about that. Perhaps different people shared their story of how Jesus had touched them. And I'm sure that more than one wanted to know the details from Lazarus about his resurrection: "Lazarus, what did you see on the other side? What was it like to come back to life?"

For Mary, spending time at His feet changed her perspective.

Mary was moved by the Spirit to do something unusual, outstanding, and even extravagant to demonstrate her total devotion to Christ. So, Mary came bearing this imported perfume, probably from India. This most likely would have been a family heirloom. However, she didn't just sprinkle a few drops of it on Jesus. With complete abandon, she poured the entire bottle on His feet, and then wiped them with her hair. The whole room would have been fragrant with the aroma from this act of complete devotion and adoration.

I think what motivated such devotion on Mary's

part was nothing less than Jesus himself. She
felt, and rightly so, there was nothing too good to
give Him—no leftovers for Him. It was only the
best. What amazes me about Mary is that she did
not have the privilege of spending as much time
in Jesus' physical presence as the apostles did.
She didn't personally hear all His teachings. But
whenever He was around, she would stop what
she was doing and listen and absorb every single
detail—the expression on His face, the nuance in
His voice, and of course, His every word. She didn't
want to miss a thing. Sure, she could have helped
her sister Martha in the kitchen. But how often do
you have the privilege of sitting at the feet of the
Creator? How often can you hear the Word of God
spoken by the Word of God himself (see John
1:1, 14)?

Mary had a perception that no one else seemed
to have. She listened in rapt attention as the Lord
spoke to the group that had gathered in Simon's
home. But with an intuition often inherent in
women, she saw and heard something else. She
saw the lines etching his face and read correctly
the problems reflected in His eyes. An inner sense
told her the disciples were wrong in expecting an

earthly kingdom. They had asked Him about it, even wondering what positions they might hold when He established it. But Jesus continued to speak of a death: His death. He told them how he would be betrayed and crucified. This simply did not compute with them, at least at the time. But Mary, her mind illuminated by the Holy Spirit, seemed to understand. The Master meant exactly what He had said. He was not speaking metaphorically; He literally was going to Jerusalem to be crucified.

Our service always should be an overflow of our worship.

She couldn't understand something so terrible, but she accepted it because He said it. She would not wait to pay a floral tribute at His funeral. She would bring her flowers now. She would give the very best she possibly could. So she lavished the beautiful and costly perfume on Jesus.

How is it that Mary had this incredible spiritual perception? Perhaps it was because of her willingness to set aside all practicality to be close to Him, to stop what she was doing, choose what was better, and simply sit at His feet.

Danish sculptor Thors Walden captured this idea well in a life-sized granite carving of Jesus. Walden sculpted the body of Christ in such a way that His face cannot be seen from a standing position. A sign next to the sculpture reads, "If you want to see the face of Jesus, you must sit at His feet." And sure enough, those who sit at the foot of the statue can look up and see the face of Jesus perfectly.

"That all sounds very spiritual," you may be thinking, "but I don't know what it means to 'sit at His feet.' That was great for those in the first century who were with Jesus in person, but I live in the twenty-first century."

Jesus is still speaking in our time as well. And we can still sit at His feet. But to do so, we need to consider Mary's devotion. If you, like Mary, want to be a spiritually insightful person, then you must first learn to be a spiritually *listening* person. For example, when you come to God in prayer, does "watch and pray" mean looking at your watch as you're talking with Him? When you open the Bible, do you really believe it is the very Word of God, sent from heaven? When you listen to the sermon at church, are you expecting to hear from God?

FROM ADORATION TO ACTION

For Mary, spending time at His feet changed her perspective, and she wanted to do something for Him. Pious platitudes may be fine for some, but Mary wanted to show her love in a tangible way. And when you truly have been sitting at His feet, you will want to serve Him too. From time to time, I hear the story of someone who is leaving their ministry because they claim to be "burned out." Frankly, I have a hard time understanding this.

Yes, I get tired *in* the Lord's work, but I never tire *of* it. I absolutely love speaking and writing and communicating the life-changing message of God's Word. Writing this book was a complete joy. It is my absolute privilege.

Our service always should be an overflow of our worship. So if our intake is less than our output, then our upkeep will be our downfall.

She who had seen Jesus was willing to do anything she could for Him. After all, He had raised her brother from the dead. Prior to that, she had lost all hope. But here Lazarus was now, alive and sitting there with her. There was no way to ever repay a debt like that. So she no doubt decided to give the most precious thing she had. But it wasn't the gift that was so significant as much as the attitude behind it. It wasn't the cost that was so important, but what it cost her.

━━━━━◦◦◦◦━━━━━

Often the people who complain the most are the ones who do the least.

━━━━━◦◦◦◦━━━━━

Not everyone appreciated her generosity and sacrifice, however:

> But one of His disciples, Judas Iscariot, Simon's son, who would betray Him, said, "Why was this fragrant oil not sold for three hundred denarii and given to the poor?" This he said, not that he cared for the poor, but because he was a thief, and had the money box; and he used to take what was put in it. But Jesus said, "Let her alone; she has kept this for the day of My burial. For the poor you have with you always, but Me you do not have always." (vv. 4–8)

Judas, a man who knew the price of everything and the value of nothing, instantly calculated the waste, which in terms of today's economy, would have been twenty-five to thirty-five thousand dollars. Certainly that was and is a very large amount of money.

Mark's Gospel tells us, "But there were some

who were indignant among themselves" (14:4). On the surface, it seemed like a legitimate complaint. Was this practical? Was it good stewardship?

But John tells us what was *really* going on: "This he said, not that he cared for the poor, but because he was a thief, and had the money box; and he used to take what was put in it" (v. 6). Ironically, it was just after this that Judas approached the chief priests with his plan of betrayal.

WILL THE REAL BELIEVER PLEASE STAND UP?

Judas' attitude is typical of that of so many people today. Like dutiful Pharisees, many will give only what is required by God. They will try to get by with the bare minimum, asking themselves, "What is the least I can do and still technically be a Christian?" They will go to church, but just once a week is satisfactory. They will read the Bible for a few minutes a day, if they can find the time. They will pray briefly before meals and before bed. They will put something in the offering—if they have any spare change. And then to add insult to injury, they will criticize others who do more!

I have noticed over the years that often the people who complain the most are the ones who do the least, while those who complain the least are the ones who do the most. And frequently the criticism will tell you more about the people themselves than those whom they are criticizing. When you hear someone harping on the same sin over and over again, it just may be the very sin that person is guilty of.

This was true in Judas' case. He didn't care for the poor. His motives were greed and selfishness. "It was a waste!" Judas complained. Yet in a few hours, Jesus would call Judas "the son of perdition," or literally, "the son of waste."

Judas never was a true believer, although he could be found in the company of the other disciples. He appeared to be a spiritual man, especially when he made a statement like this one. But things are not always as they seem. At this moment, Mary may have seemed wasteful and frivolous because of her gift, while Judas appeared to be thrifty, compassionate, and spiritual.

Yet in realty, Mary was the one who was spiritual and sacrificial, while Judas was wicked and greedy. Mary would spare no expense, because she had a glimpse of what Jesus had really come to do: "to give His life a ransom for many" (Matt. 20:28).

In Mark's account of the same event, Jesus

186 | Deepening Your Faith

answered Judas by saying, "She has done what she could. She has come beforehand to anoint My body for burial. Assuredly, I say to you, wherever this gospel is preached in the whole world, what this woman has done will also be told as a memorial to her" (Mark 14:8–9). Mary did what she could because she understood that Jesus would do what He did.

Nothing is ever wasted when it is done from a right motive for the glory of God.

GIVING OUR BEST

The more we know of what Jesus did for us, the more we will want to do for Him. Nothing is ever wasted when it is done from a right motive for the glory of God. In the eyes of unbelievers, what we Christians do may seem wasteful and silly. *Why go to church all the time, especially on a Wednesday night to some midweek study? Isn't Sunday morning enough? Why read Christian books? Why feed the homeless? Why go halfway around the world to preach to someone who may not even listen? You can't save everyone.*

We do these things because we all have a part to play in the advancement of God's kingdom. Mary did what she could, and we must do what we can. She couldn't do everything, but she could do something. In the same way, you can't do everything, but you can do something. You can't win everyone in the world to Jesus Christ, but you can win some. As it has been said, "I am only one, but I am one. I cannot do everything, but I can do something. What I can do, I ought to do, and what I ought to do, by the grace of God, I will do!" We must all do what we can, while we can.

When a believer gives up a promising career to become a missionary in a remote part of the world, some will say, "What a waste!"

When you give up certain pleasures and activities because you don't want to dull your spiritual life, some will say, "What a waste! You missed out big time!"

When you have been faithful to your spouse throughout your marriage, have honored your vows, and have refused to give in to the temptation to go astray, some will say, "What a waste! You could have been on your third marriage by now!"

When you recognize that the work of God's

kingdom is worth investing in and you give faithfully and regularly of your time and money, some will say, "What a waste!"

Or, you may decide to simply live for yourself and do whatever you want to with your life. Then God will say, "What a waste!"

*You can't do everything,
but you can do something.*

Whose opinion do you care about most: God's? Or this world's? Like Mary, could it be said of you that you did what you could? If so, you will never regret it. Your only regret will be that you didn't do more. When you come to the end of your life and look back, what will you see? Will you regret the fact that you didn't use the gifts and talents God gave you in service to Him? God will not hold you accountable for what He called others to do. He will hold you accountable for what He called you to do.

The Bible tells us there is coming a day of judgment for Christians in this very area:

> For no one can lay any foundation other than the one already laid, which is Jesus Christ. If any man builds on this foundation using gold, silver, costly stones, wood, hay

or straw, his work will be shown for what it
is, because the Day will bring it to light. It
will be revealed with fire, and the fire will
test the quality of each man's work. If what
he has built survives, he will receive his
reward. If it is burned up, he will suffer loss;
he himself will be saved, but only as one
escaping through the flames.
(1 Cor. 3:11–15 NIV)

This passage is telling us that two classes of
believers will stand at the judgment seat of Christ.
First, there will be those who built on the right
foundation using, gold, silver, and gems. These
are the believers who invested their lives and used
their time and money wisely. And they will be
rewarded.

Then there will be those who built on the wrong
foundation, who didn't do anything of great value
for God with the time and resources He gave them,
but still they will be saved. These believers will
have a saved soul, but a lost life.

This will not be a judgment concerning our
salvation, because that has been given to us when
we responded to the gospel and put our faith in
Christ. Rather, this judgment has to do with how
our believing the gospel has affected our lives—

what it has resulted in. Speaking to believers, the apostle Paul wrote, "For we must all appear before the judgment seat of Christ, that each one may receive the things done in the body, according to what he has done, whether good or bad" (2 Cor. 5:10).

A person's actions form an infallible index to his or her character. Jesus said, "By their fruits you will know them" (Matt. 7:20).

THE STORY OF TWO MILLIONAIRES

As a graduation gift from his parents, William Borden, heir to the Borden dairy estate, received a trip around the world. As he traveled through Asia, the Middle East, and Europe, he felt a growing burden for people who did not know the Lord. Finally, he wrote home to say, "I'm going to give my life to prepare for the mission field." Upon making his decision, he wrote two words in the back of his Bible: "NO RESERVES."

Upon graduation from Yale, Borden turned down some high-paying job offers. But he was determined to fulfill the call God had placed on his life. He wrote two more words in the back of his Bible: "NO RETREAT." Borden went on to do graduate work at Princeton Seminary, and upon completing his studies, he sailed for China to work with Muslims. But first, he stopped in Egypt to study Arabic. While he was there, he came down with spinal meningitis. And within a month, twenty-five-year-old William Borden was dead. In the back of his Bible, two more words had been written: "NO REGRETS."

No reserves. No retreat. No regrets. These six words encompassed the principles of William Borden's life.

Contrast Borden's life with that of millionaire Howard Hughes. The film about his life, *The Aviator*, chronicles his amazing achievements in aviation and other exploits. Yet a few important details were left out, including the fact that Hughes was a very immoral man who had been involved with many, many women. In *The Aviator*, Hughes' eccentricities were attributed to a vague form of mental illness, triggered by his mother's behavior.

The real Howard Hughes contracted syphilis, no doubt from his philandering, which attacked his brain in the form of neurosyphilis, causing him to go insane. Where the drugs ended and the disease began, however, is anyone's guess. His autopsy revealed dozens of needle tips that had broken off and had lodged in his arms and legs.

*Mary did what she could,
and we must do what we can.*

He spent the last two decades of his life bedridden and alone in a hotel room, covered in his own excrement. Having survived on a diet of candy and cake, he had lost all his teeth, and his fingernails were so long that they curved under his fingers.

Hughes took his last breath on a plane heading back to the U.S. from Mexico. Afterward, the few people who had been loyal to him went to war for his estate, creating several fake wills to bolster their greed.

In contrast to William Borden, Howard Hughes had many regrets, I'm sure. But you won't see a movie about William Borden. His life didn't have the sizzle or the sex appeal of Howard Hughes' life. Nor did it have the same ending. William Borden is in heaven. And where is Howard Hughes? Only God knows.

A life is never wasted when it is invested in

bringing people to Jesus. Nor is it wasted when it is lived for the glory of God. But it is wasted when it is lived for selfish ambition.

We need to follow the example of people like William Borden and Mary. We need to do what we can. God has given each of us influence, opportunities, resources, and time. Let's choose what is best so that we can say of our lives: No reserves. No retreat. No regrets.

9   FINDERS, WEEPERS; LOSERS, KEEPERS

John 12:12–25

What makes us happy? *Time's* January 17, 2005 cover story, "The New Science of Happiness," offered some surprising answers to that question. Happiness isn't found in the places many people would expect to find it. "Research has shown that once your basic needs are met, additional income does little to raise your sense of satisfaction," the article said.[1] Is it a good education, then? No. A high IQ? No. How about youth? No again. In fact, older people are consistently more satisfied with their lives than the young.

An article from the same issue entitled, "The Real Truth about Money," states, "If you made a graph of American life since the end of World War II, every line concerning money and the things money can buy would soar upward. But if you made a chart of American happiness since the end of World War II, the lines would be as flat as a marble tabletop."[2]

So if we don't find happiness in wealth, youth, or education, where *do* we find it? Let me first tell you where we *won't* find it. It will not come from this world. The fleeting happiness this world has to offer comes and goes, depending on our circumstances. If things are going reasonably well, we are happy. If they are not, then we are unhappy. But we need to remember, "There are two sources of unhappiness in life. One is not getting what you want. The other is getting it."

This was true of a lottery winner named Jack Whittaker:

> Jewel Whittaker, wife of the lottery winner who took home the richest undivided jackpot in U.S. history—a lump-sum payout of about $113 million after taxes—now says she regrets his purchase of the ticket that won the $314.9 million jackpot. Since winning two years ago, her husband, Jack Whittaker, 57, of West Virginia has been arrested twice for driving under the influence and ordered into rehab, faces charges that he attacked a bar manager, and is accused in two lawsuits of making trouble at a nightclub and a racetrack.[3]

So be careful what you wish for. Money can buy us some things, but not the most important things.

Money can buy you a bed, but not sleep; books, but not brains; a house, but not a home; medicine, but not health; finery, but not beauty; and amusement, but not happiness. And to quote Sir Paul, John, George, and Ringo, "Money can't buy you love."

The fleeting happiness this world has to offer comes and goes.

So where do we find the meaning and purpose in life that we all crave? How can we be truly happy people? In the *Time* article and elsewhere, an interesting fact was mentioned regarding the search for happiness: Scandinavians were the happiest people on Earth, followed by the Americans at a close second. Faith, family, and friends all contributed to happiness. According to *Time*, "Love, friendship, family … the belief that your life has purpose—these are the essentials of human fulfillment, and they can't be purchased with cash."[4]

Those of us who weren't born into a Scandinavian family can't do much about that. But the belief that our lives have purpose—that's something we can work with.

THE ROAD TO HAPPINESS

Does your life have purpose? According to the Bible, if we seek to know God and discover His plan for our lives, then we will find the happiness that has eluded us for so long. Happiness comes not as a result of seeking it, but seeking Him. Psalm 144:15 says, "Happy are the people whose God is the Lord!" And as C. S. Lewis observed, "God designed the human machine to run on Himself."[5]

According to Scripture, happiness is never something that should be sought directly. It is always something that results from seeking something else. If we seek holiness, we'll find happiness. Jesus said, "Blessed are those who hunger and thirst for righteousness, for they shall be filled" (Matt. 5:6). The word "blessed" in this verse also could be translated, "happy." As our will becomes aligned with God's, and as we walk in harmony with Him, the other areas of our lives will find their proper balance. We find what we are looking for in life not by seeking it in and of itself, but by seeking God. Henry Ward Beecher said, "The strength and the happiness of a man consists in finding out the way in which God is going, and going in that way too."

"WE WISH TO SEE JESUS."

Two thousand years ago, there were some Greek men who wanted to meet Jesus. Perhaps it was their disillusionment with their pagan ways that sent them searching. Perhaps they had heard that Jesus raised people from the dead. It may have been mere curiosity. Whatever the case, Jesus revealed to them—and to us—the meaning and purpose of life, the secret to living a happy and meaningful life. John records their story for us:

> Now there were certain Greeks among those who came up to worship at the feast. Then they came to Philip, who was from Bethsaida of Galilee, and asked him, saying, "Sir, we wish to see Jesus." Philip came and told Andrew, and in turn Andrew and Philip told Jesus. (12:20–22)

This inquiry from these Greeks trigged an important event in Jesus' life. They approached Philip, perhaps because he had a Greek name. Philip then brought the request to Andrew, who told Jesus. But something about these men and their request drew this response from Jesus: "The hour has come that the Son of Man should be glorified" (v. 23).

What was this "hour" Jesus spoke of? It was the hour of His crucifixion. On many occasions prior to this, He would resist the pressure of others to completely reveal himself. He would say, "My hour has not yet come." But now it had. These Greek men were but the beginning of millions who would follow, who would find life because of His death on the cross for the whole world.

Happiness comes not as a result of seeking it, but seeking Him.

But why would these men come to Jesus in the first place? Historically, Greece at this time was the center of human wisdom, the fountainhead of philosophy, the matrix of mythology, and the cradle of civilized society. It was an open and free society, devoid of absolutes, where people were encouraged to live as they please. Immorality was pervasive, marriage was crumbling, and justice was lacking. These men most likely had chased after the promises of hedonism and came back empty-handed. (It sounds a lot like our nation today, doesn't it?)

So, they came to Jerusalem looking for answers.

It reminds me of another searching group who went to Jerusalem: The wise men from the East, who said, "Where is He who has been born King of the Jews?" (Matt. 2:2), as well as the Ethiopian who had come to Jerusalem in search of God (see Acts 8:27). When these Greeks arrived in the city, the place was abuzz for Passover. The name of Jesus was on everyone's lips. So they decided they would try to see Jesus. To them, and to all of us, Jesus revealed what they were searching for: the meaning of life, the secret of happiness.

THE GREAT PARADOX

But it wasn't what we might expect: "Most assuredly, I say to you, unless a grain of wheat falls into the ground and dies, it remains alone; but if it dies, it produces much grain. He who loves his life will lose it, and he who hates his life in this world will keep it for eternal life" (vv. 24–25). Now this flies in the face of conventional wisdom. *He who loves his life will lose it.* ... This seems so hard to understand, so unnatural, and so impossible. But when you stop and think about it, it makes complete sense.

Think of all the people who are trying to live

life to its fullest, but are going about it in the wrong way. They think it's ridiculous to wait until marriage to engage in sexual activity. And if you are married and the thrill is gone, spice it up and have an affair, they say. If your spouse finds out, just terminate the marriage and move on. If you want to get ahead in school, just cheat here and there, but don't get caught. If you want to get a good job, exaggerate about your experience on that résumé. File that false claim to get an insurance payout. If someone bothers you, sue them. When those taxes are due, lie to save some money. The list goes on and on—and so do the repercussions.

Jesus revealed what they were searching for: the meaning of life.

But God's wisdom says that if you love your life, you will lose it. If you live for yourself, you never will really find yourself. God's plan for you to find meaning, purpose, and yes, happiness, is this: lose your life to find it. This isn't always easy to do, because it means you have to let go. You have to submit to the will of God for your life.

Of course, we don't always know the will of

God in every given situation. And then there are times when we know it, but we don't like it, as was the case with Jonah. Or, it doesn't make sense, just as it didn't for Joseph or Job. Yet we must never be afraid to place an unknown future into the hands of a known God. D. L. Moody said, "Spread out your petition before God, and then say, 'Thy will, not mine, be done.' The sweetest lesson I have learned in God's school is to let the Lord choose for me." Would you be willing to take your future, place it in God's hands, and "let the Lord choose for you"? If you are willing, then you will discover that the Christian life is paradoxical in so many ways. What we really want will not come by the ways this world teaches us.

Everyone wants more power in their lives, from the most powerful computer to the most powerful car to the most powerful position or the most powerful body. After all, we reason, with power, we can rule, influence, and control. So God says, "You want power? Here's how to get it: you will find it in weakness." God said to the apostle Paul, "My grace is sufficient for you, for My strength is made perfect in weakness" (2 Cor. 12:9). *If you lose your life, you will find it.*

Leaders want others to listen to what they have to say and to follow their leadership. But Jesus says, "You want to lead? Learn first to follow and serve." Speaking in Mark 9:35, Jesus said, "If anyone desires to be first, he shall be last of all and servant of all." *If you lose your life, you will find it.*

We want our marriages to be successful, but it won't come through the conventional wisdom of a fifty-fifty commitment. No, it's a one hundred-one hundred commitment. Without any thought of our own gain, we must put our spouse's needs above our own. Husbands, do you want your wives to submit to you? Then God says, "Love your wives, just as Christ also loved the church and gave Himself for her" (Eph. 5:25). Wives, do you want your husband to be a spiritual leader? Then "submit to your own husbands, as to the Lord" (Eph. 5:22). *If you lose your life, you will find it.*

In the Christian life, the way to greatness is through humility, the way to power is through weakness, the way to life is through death, and the way up is down. And let me add one more: the way to happiness is misery. Jesus said, "Blessed are those who mourn, for they shall be comforted" (Matt. 5:4). Or, "happy are the unhappy." As I wrote earlier, the word "blessed" could also be translated "happy." It originates from the Greek word, *makariôs*, which was a Mediterranean island of Cyprus. Because of its geographical location, balmy climate, and fertile soil, the Greeks believed that anyone who lived on this island had it made in the shade. They believed everything needed for happiness and fulfillment was found there.

Never be afraid to place an unknown future into the hands of a known God.

No need to import anything—you had it all on this self-contained island of bliss. This was a metaphor for what blessedness, or happiness, is. Jesus was saying, blessedness, or true happiness, is independent from circumstances. In other words, blessedness, the happiness that God has for you, is independent of what is happening to you.

THE DO'S AND DON'TS OF A HAPPY LIFE

So does this mean that to find life and happiness, we must live a miserable, restricted life? No. But having said that, it does mean that to be happy, there are things we should and should not do. Psalm 1 speaks of how to live a happy life: "Blessed is the man who walks not in the counsel of the ungodly, nor stands in the path of sinners, nor sits in the seat of the scornful" (v. 1). God begins this psalm not with the power of positive thinking, but with the power of negative thinking. He is telling us that the one who would be a happy, happy person should begin by avoiding certain things that make it impossible for happiness to flourish. These things are poisonous and counterproductive. Therefore, you begin by avoiding the influence of ungodly people who would persuade you to do ungodly things: "Blessed is the man who walks not in the counsel of the ungodly. ... " So happiness is found in what we *don't* do.

But it is also found it what we *do*. Psalm 1 continues, "But his delight is in the law of the Lord, and in His law he meditates day and night. He shall be like a tree planted by the rivers of water, that brings forth its fruit in its season, whose leaf also shall not wither; and whatever he does shall prosper" (vv. 2–3). The happy person of Psalm 1 stays in God's Word. Amazingly, at the time this psalm was written, "the law of the Lord" consisted only of the first five Books of Moses. So how much more should we Christians today practice meditating on God's Word? After all, we have sixty-six books to read! For this happy person, to look into God's Word was a joy. This verse doesn't say, "His drudgery is in the law of the Lord," or "His dread is in the law of the Lord." Not even "His duty is in the law of the Lord," although one could make a case for the dutiful study of Scripture.

True happiness is independent from circumstances.

This verse also says the happy man meditates in the law of the Lord "day and night" (v. 2). We need to read the Bible in a methodical, meaningful, meditative way, asking certain questions when we are meditating on God's Word:

- Is there any *sin* here for me to avoid?
- Is there any *promise* for me to claim?
- Is there any *victory* to gain?
- Is there any *blessing* to enjoy?

Thus, we see from these verses that happiness is found in being both *reactive* and *proactive*. We are both resisting what is wrong *and* embracing what is right. If we do this, the Bible says we will find happiness.

This is the great Christian paradox. In fact, if this element is not present, then it is not the authentic gospel, because the gospel begins with a cross. If you hear a so-called gospel proclaimed from a pulpit, on TV, or on the radio, and that gospel does not begin with a cross and the fact that some part of you has to die, then it is not the true gospel. If it tells you to believe, but not to repent, then it is not the true gospel. If it promises heaven, but does not warn of hell, then it is not the true gospel.

The gospel begins with a cross.

There is the prosperity gospel of today that says you can have it all. You don't have to be sick or in debt; you can be a champion. But Jesus says that if you are living to please and find yourself, you will lose yourself. This means that we must see ourselves for what we really are. We need to realize that living for ourselves never will supply what we really want out of life.

Remember, Jesus said, "He who loves his life will lose it, he who hates his life in this world will keep it for eternal life" (v. 25). Only when Jesus

Christ is in total control of your life, only when God becomes your everything and self becomes nothing, only when your love for God is so great that your self-love seems like hate in comparison, only then will you truly find yourself.

DYING DAILY

The cross of Christ stands for two things in our lives. It stands for a once-and-for-all decision to commit our lives to Christ as Savior and Lord. And it stands for a daily, continual series of choices. We must not only surrender to Jesus once; we must surrender repeatedly, moment by moment, day by day. Every minute of every day, we must renew our own commitment to Christ. If you belong to Jesus, every day will have its cross. Every day will have something you *ought* to do, but don't feel like doing. Every day will have something you *should not* do, but want to do. That is your cross. Every day, we have to die a little to live for Jesus. Paul said, "I die daily" (1 Cor. 15:31), and Jesus said, "If anyone desires to come after Me, let him deny himself, and take up his cross daily, and follow Me" (Luke 9:23). This is a foundational issue.

We essentially have a choice in life: to live for ourselves or deny ourselves; to ignore the cross or take it up; to seek to save our lives and ultimately lose them; to lose our lives and ultimately find them; to gain the world or to forsake the world; to lose our souls or to keep them; to share His reward and glory or to lose it.

Every day, we have to die a little to live for Jesus.

When Jesus said, "Whoever loses his life for My sake will save it" (Luke 9:24), the Greek word He used for "life" was *psuché*, meaning, "soul life"—our wills, ambition, goals, and desires. In other words, Jesus was saying that if we seek to be happy, then we never will be. But if we will lose (or invest and commit) our lives to Him, then we will be happy. We must continually dedicate to Him our lives, our families, our ministries, our possessions, our careers, our plans, and our futures.

But sometimes we are afraid to do that. We think God has it in for us, and once we make that commitment, we are done for. But in reality, that is a warped concept of God. We need to know that

God's plans are better than our plans for ourselves, as Jeremiah 29:11 promises: "For I know the thoughts that I think toward you, says the Lord, thoughts of peace and not of evil, to give you a future and a hope."

GOD'S PLAN FOR US

God instructed His priests to pronounce this blessing on His people time and time again: "The Lord bless you and keep you; the Lord make His face shine upon you, and be gracious to you; the Lord lift up His countenance upon you, and give you peace" (Num. 6:24–26).

First, this blessing would remind them God wanted to bless them (v. 24). It is God's very delight to bless you over and over again. Jesus said, "For it is your Father's good pleasure to give you the kingdom" (Luke 12:32).

Second, this blessing would remind them that God would keep them (v. 24). The word "keep" used in this verse was a Hebrew word that means, "to keep, to watch, to guard, to hedge about." You don't lose something you love. You don't go to Disneyland with your children and completely forget about them and leave. God will not always keep you *from* testing, but He will keep you *in* it.

Third, this blessing would remind them that God wanted to smile on them (v. 25). God wants to be reminded daily that when He looks on us, He smiles. That is what this text means. Sadly, that is not the picture many people have of the Lord. They see Him as a frowning Father in Heaven who is rarely, if ever, pleased by us. But that is not the picture that God gives us of himself. God's face shines with pleasure toward us as His people. When He sees you, His face lights up with joy.

Fourth, this blessing would remind them that God is gracious to them (v. 25). God does not deal with us according to His justice, but according to His grace.

Fifth, this blessing would remind them that God is attentive to them (v. 26). The phrase, "lift up His countenance" from verse 26 literally means, "to look, to see, to know, to be interested, to have one's full attention." God is saying, "I watch out for you each and every day, and you have My full attention!" Have you ever been speaking to someone and pouring out your heart, and they are looking past you? It's very disheartening. Sometimes we may wonder if God is paying

attention to us, if He knows what is happening
in our lives. The Bible tells us that He is paying
attention; He does know.

*God's plans are better than
our plans for ourselves.*

*Sixth, this blessing would remind them that
He wants to give them His peace (v. 26).* As we
consider the fact that the Lord wants to bless us,
keep us, and smile on us, it should give us personal
peace. When we consider that God is both gracious
and attentive to us, we should be at peace.

So here is God's plan for you, better than
anything you have ever envisioned for yourself. It
is a plan to make your life meaningful, purposeful,
happy, and contented, with the promise of heaven
someday: *If you lose your life, you will find it.*

We've heard the expression, "Finders, keepers;
losers, weepers." According to Jesus, it should be,
"Finders, weepers; losers, keepers." The way up is
down. The way to find life is by losing it. The way to
happiness is misery.

Do you want this happiness? Do you want to
know the meaning of life? It comes only through

the cross: " 'Most assuredly, I say to you, unless a grain of wheat falls into the ground and dies, it remains alone; but if it dies, it produces much grain' " (John 6:24). Jesus was that "grain of wheat" that would go into the ground and die. And through His death, life came to all of us.

Notes

Chapter 3: Breakfast with Jesus

1. John Stossel, "The Mystery of Happiness," *ABC Special Report*, ABC, September 4, 1997.

2. Albert Benjamin Simpson, *The Best of A. B. Simpson*, Keith M. Bailey, comp. (Camp Hill, Pa.: Christian Publications, 1987).

Chapter 5: Believing Is Seeing

1. Rod Dreher, "God Bless Ted Turner," *National Review Online*, February 11, 2003. http://www.nationalreview.com/script/printpage.p?ref=/dreher/dreher021103.asp.

2. C. S. Lewis, *The Problem of Pain* (San Francisco: HarperSan Francisco, 2001), 91.

3. Interview by Larry King, *Larry King Live*, CNN, August 4, 2005.

Chapter 6: An Abundant Life

1. Phillip Keller, *A Shepherd Looks at Psalm 23* (Grand Rapids, Mich.: Zondervan Publishing House, 1970), 35.

Chapter 7: Right on Time

1. Thomas N. Heymann, *In an Average Lifetime* (New York: Ballantine Books, 1991).

Chapter 8: No Regrets

1. Maureen Cleave, *London Evening Standard*, March 4, 1966.

2. Brian Lewis, "The Popular Jesus Is Emerging," *The Tennessean*, January 25, 2004.

Chapter 9: Finders, Weepers; Losers, Keepers

1. Claudia Wallis, "The New Science of Happiness," *Time*, January 17, 2005.

2. Gregg Easterbrook, "The Real Truth about Money," *Time*, January 17, 2005.

3. Craig Wilson, "How Much Would Make You Smile?" USA Today.com, December 26, 2004. http://yahoo.usatoday.com/life/lifestyle/2004-12-26-money-happiness_x.htm?csp=1.

4. Wallis, "The New Science of Happiness."

5. C. S. Lewis, *Mere Christianity* (San Francisco: HarperSan Francisco, 2001), 50.

About the Author

Greg Laurie is the pastor of Harvest Christian Fellowship (one of America's largest churches) in Riverside, California. He is the author of over thirty books, including the Gold Medallion Award winner, *The Upside-Down Church*, as well as *Every Day with Jesus*; *Are We Living in the Last Days?*; *Marriage Connections*; and *Losers and Winners, Saints and Sinners*. You can find his study notes in the New Believer's Bible and the Seeker's Bible. Host of the *Harvest: Greg Laurie* television program and the nationally syndicated radio program, *A New Beginning, Greg Laurie* is also the founder and featured speaker for Harvest Crusades—contemporary, large-scale evangelistic outreaches, which local churches organize nationally and internationally. He and his wife Cathe have two children and live in Southern California.